Searching For Heroes In Life is a Christian-themed memoir that examines the need for heroes, and how to find them. In his book the author calls a "testimonial journey," he discusses his lifelong experience of finding heroes who either directly inspired or directly helped him.

For readers who are looking for an amalgam of spiritual guidance, encouragement, and Christian theology, this is a touching lesson in the debts we all owe to others. It is an affecting, humble critique of unrestrained individualism.

(Kirkus Reviews)

Searching

for

Heroes

in

Life

Charles Brookins Taylor, Sr.

WESTBOW
PRESS®
A DIVISION OF THOMAS NELSON
& ZONDERVAN

All Scripture quotations are from *Today's Parallel Bible*, copyright 2000, by the
Zondervan Publishing Corporation. Used by permission. All rights reserved.

Verses marked KJV are from The Holy Bible, King James Version.
Verses marked NIV are from The Holy Bible, New International Version.
Verses marked NLT are from The Holy Bible, New Living Translation.
Verses marked NASB are from The Holy Bible, New American Standard Bible.

WestBow Press books may be ordered through booksellers or by contacting:

WestBow Press
A Division of Thomas Nelson & Zondervan
1663 Liberty Drive
Bloomington, IN 47403
www.westbowpress.com
1 (866) 928-1240

Because of the dynamic nature of the Internet, any web addresses or
links contained in this book may have changed since publication and
may no longer be valid. The views expressed in this work are solely those
of the author and do not necessarily reflect the views of the publisher,
and the publisher hereby disclaims any responsibility for them.

Any people depicted in stock imagery provided by Thinkstock are
models, and such images are being used for illustrative purposes only.
Certain stock imagery © Thinkstock.

ISBN: 978-1-4908-7879-9 (sc)
ISBN: 978-1-4908-7881-2 (hc)
ISBN: 978-1-4908-7880-5 (e)

Library of Congress Control Number: 2015907074

Print information available on the last page.

WestBow Press rev. date: 08/01/2017

This book is dedicated with love to my father, the late Oscar Taylor Sr.; my mother, the late Rosa Brookins Taylor, who taught me the power of faith and the dignity of labor; and my God, for His faithfulness and strength.

CONTENTS

ACKNOWLEDGMENTS

I'd like to thank my wife, Carolyn, a former teacher and a former director in the Suffolk County, New York, Department of Social Services. She is a forty-two-year breast cancer survivor. I thank her for her able assistance, guidance, suggestions, and loving encouragement both in my life and on this project. Surely, she is my constant hero.

Thanks also to my sons and daughters, who, in their own individual ways, inspired me along this journey.

Finally, I would like to thank my publisher, WestBow Press, a Division of Thomas Nelson & Zondervan, and their many representatives and staff members who guided me through the process of writing this book for publication.

INTRODUCTION

We search for heroes throughout our lifelong journey. It requires us to look both within and without. Each one of us must search for our own heroes. The more we search, the more we begin to live a life of gratitude, giving thanks for those heroes who have had a positive influence in our lives.

Searching for heroes in our lives cannot be approached casually. It is like searching for pearls: we can find them if we dig deep enough. And search we must, for we cannot reach our full potential without heroes.

The first step in this search is to understand what a hero is. How do we define a hero? According to *The New Shorter Oxford English Dictionary, Fourth Edition, Vol. 1, 1993,* a hero is a person recognized or admired for his or her courage, ability, or achievements and noble qualities in any field. The next question we need to ask is how we recognize a hero. Recognizing someone is an act of acknowledgment or admission of a service or achievement; to recognize is accord notice or attention, to show appreciation of service or achievement.

Why is it so difficult to recognize heroes in our lives? In part, it's because we live in a society that is primarily driven by the ideal of self-centeredness and focuses on *me, myself, and I,* one that is described as individualism. But the fact is, the more we search, the more we will realize that each one of us needs heroes, because no one is an island unto himself.

Too often we forget that throughout our life journey there are many heroes along the way who have gone unrecognized. If only we would take time out and pause for a moment and reflect on our lives, we would surely discover that many of these heroes have gone unrecognized. Yet these heroes have helped us navigate through the "hierarchical stages of need" in our lives, influencing us in positive ways.

Another reason we have not recognized heroes in our life journey is that by and large, we have allowed society to define our heroes for us. Think about it: we have not only allowed the media to define our heroes for us, but we have also allowed it and other facets of our society to establish the parameters or boundaries by which a hero is defined. Therefore, we too often look for heroes in the wrong places and in the wrong way. As a result, we fail to look beneath the "rim," beyond the sports arena or the political arena, and yes, beyond Tinseltown. In short, one does not have to be able to jump above a basketball rim and dunk a basketball, does not have to possess extraordinary physical prowess, does not have to possess extraordinary mental capacity, or gain riches or fame in this world in order to be a hero. It is my belief that as we widen our search for heroes, we will find real heroes in our everyday lives who have influenced us in positive ways.

I suggest that you define your own heroes by using the definition given earlier as a guideline. Why is this so important? First of all, until you understand how and why someone is your hero, you cannot begin to recognize true heroes in your life. And secondly, each one of us experiences them through our five natural senses and, yes, through our spiritual sense, throughout our life journey. As a result, you, as an individual, determine which people have influenced your life in a positive way. We need to take time out of our hectic schedules and find a place of solitude and reflect on our lives. When we do this, we will begin to discover our real heroes in a true sense.

Our Ultimate Needs in Life Cannot Be Realized Without Heroes

Everyone has needs, and everyone needs others to help meet those needs. According to Abraham Maslow's Hierarchy of Needs, there are five levels of needs. He believed that people have an inborn desire to be self-actualized, to be all they can be. He believed that we move from the basic to more complex needs. This hierarchy of needs is most often displayed as a pyramid that shows physiological needs as the most basic ones, the foundation of all other needs

(About.com Psychology, cited, March 30, 2015 at *http://psychology. about.com/od/theoriesofpersonality/a/hierarachyneeds.htm*).

The following is a list of Maslow's five levels of needs and a brief summary of each:

1. Physiological Needs
    These needs are said to be the most basic and are vital to survival: water, air, food, and sleep. Maslow believed that all other needs become secondary until these physiological needs are met.

2. Security Needs
    These are the needs for safety and security. They are important for survival but are not as demanding as the physiological needs. Examples of security needs include a desire for steady employment, health care, safe neighborhoods, and shelter from the environment.

3. Social Needs

Social needs include the needs for belonging, love, and affection. Maslow described these needs as less basic than physiological and security needs. Relationship such as friendships, romantic attachments, and families help fulfill the need for companionship and acceptance, as does involvement in social, community, or religious groups.

4. Esteem Needs

After the first three needs are satisfied, according to Maslow, self-esteem needs become increasingly important. These include the need for things that reflect on self-esteem, personal worth, social recognition, and a sense of accomplishment.

5. Self-Actualization Needs

According to Maslow, this is the highest level of needs and refers to a person's full potential. Maslow describes this level as the desire to accomplish everything that one can, to become the most that one can be. This level of need may focus on a personal desire. For example, a person may have the desire to become the very best athlete. Another person may have the strong desire to become an ideal parent. Others may want to express their best selves in paintings, pictures, politics, inventions, or something else. Maslow believed that to understand this level of need, the person must not only achieve the previous needs, but master them.

(Maslow's hierarchy of needs, From Wikipedia, the free encyclopedia, cited March 30, 2015, at.http://en.wikipedia.org/wiki/File:MaslowsHierchyOfNeeds.svg).

The Maslow hierarchy of needs has contributed to the fields of psychology, education, and industry, to name a few. Although I am not an avid student of psychology, I was required to take psychology courses in the school of education and in my seminary training. I believe the hierarchy should indeed be given much credence, although I am sure you are aware, as I am, that some people become successful in life in spite of being shortchanged as far as having their basic needs met in a systematic way.

Notwithstanding, it is my belief and experience that our highest form of life actualization is achieved by reaching the level of spiritual self-actualization, a sixth level of need, so to speak. It is a level that transcends the other needs yet permeates them. I believe this need must be met if we are to achieve our full purpose in life.

My greatest discovery was when I first came to the realization that I had entered the realm of spiritual self-actualization the day I committed my life to Jesus Christ as Lord and Savior and the Creator of the whole universe. It changed my whole attitude about life and its needs; it was then that I began to understand that Jesus is the source that meets all our needs, in both the natural and the spiritual realms.

Why is this so important to know? It is God who makes it possible for us to reach this level and to reap the full benefits of all our other needs being met. In essence, spiritual self-actualization begins with having a personal relationship with God.

When we allow this to happen, we can begin to hold to God's promise in Philippians 4:19 NIV, "God will meet all our needs," and know that God comes to man through man as He works through other people to help meet our needs. Each day of our life, in every moment of our life, He uses other people to help meet our needs. And if we truly take time out from our everyday hustle and bustle and reflect on what He has done for us, we will surely see many heroes in our lives, beginning with Jesus, the greatest hero.

It is my belief that everyone can find heroes if they diligently look for them. One of my greatest discoveries was when I understood what God is telling us in Jeremiah 29:13 NIV: "You will seek me and find me when you seek me with all your heart."

When you allow this to happen, you'll be surprised at how much more fulfilling and purposeful your life becomes.

This is what has happened to me. I invite you to travel with me on my testimonial journey as I reflect on my life and my searching for and finding heroes along the way. It is not my intention to give you an exhaustive picture of my life. Rather, I will highlight special events and moments, recognizing heroes who did something for me or said something to me that influenced me to go forward in a positive way, and all of whom awakened in me the power of positive thinking, producing an attitude of gratitude. As you journey with me, it is my hope that you, too, will begin to discover those heroes who have helped you go forward in life in a positive way.

CHAPTER 1

The Foundational Stage: Where Do We Begin?

Searching for heroes in life begins the day we are born. It has been said that men and women are imitative beings. From the very first day one is born, to the very last day of life here on earth, one is learning to do what one sees or hears others do. Most psychologists and educators will agree with that statement.

It is said that the foundation of a child's character is developed by the time he reaches the age of five. It's no wonder we grown-ups are told to be careful about what we say and do around children. From day one my mother and father and, yes, others around me were influencing me. The older I get, and the more I reflect on my life, the more I realize they were real heroes, although I didn't always recognize it at the time. Now I do! And I thank them more and more every day, although some of those people are no longer here.

As early as I can recall, it was my mother who first instilled in me a sense of the dignity of love for God and others and the importance of education. My mother was raised up in the home of a preacher. Her father was a preacher, and as a result, she was raised in a Christian environment. My mother also was an educator in her younger years. Before marrying my father, she taught school in a one-room schoolhouse, which was typical in the early twentieth century.

In addition to this great sense of moral value, what impressed me was how dedicated she was to my father and our family of ten children. It was my mother who cooked three meals a day for the family. It was my mother who raised chickens and eggs for us to eat. It was my mother who grew vegetables in the garden. It was my mother who often took eggs to the grocery store and sold them to the store owner so that we could buy flour, spices, and other items for her to make the best meals she could for us. Now that I look back, I'm amazed at how she managed to feed twelve people three meals every day except Sunday, a day set apart for going to church. During the weekdays she also worked in the fields with us in the early part of the day.

It was not just what she did that influenced me to move forward in life; it was also what she said. One rainy day as some of my sisters and I were walking home from school on a dirt road, someone came by in a truck. The driver steered his truck too close to us, and to avoid being hit, we had to dive into the muddy ditch. After my sisters and I crawled out of the ditch, I wiped the mud from my face, and with tears in my eyes, we headed home. When we arrived home, my mother looked at me and asked, "What happened to you!"

I replied, "Some old man riding in a truck ran us into the ditch, and I am going to get him one day, you just wait and see."

My mother reached out with her comforting arms and hugged me as she said, "You may not forget him, but you must forgive him." My mother always exuded a quiet, comforting spirit, yet it was a strong spirit. She was a "quiet fire."

My mother had a special song she would often sing as she was cooking in the kitchen: "I've Got a Key to the Kingdom." What's so amazing to me now is that when I asked my other brothers and sisters if they remembered her singing that song, they all said no. But for some reason, I did, and after I grew older and answered the call to the ministry, I was able to find the words to it, and it was then that I realized that just maybe I was the one to whom she was singing.

My father instilled in me a sense of the dignity of labor and the need to build for the future. He was the epitome of a man who was tough minded and tender hearted, a rare combination indeed.

Although he had only a fourth-grade education, he had a rich informal education, and common sense to go with it. He reminded me that as soon as he was big enough to work odd jobs, that is what he did to make a living. He said his dream was to buy a section of land that he could call his own. However, he knew that with the little money he was making in Alabama, it would take him years to buy land.

Somehow, with the help of the Lord, he was able to work his way to West Virginia to get a job working in the coal mines. He said, "It was good pay, all right, but it was hard and dangerous work." It was not just the danger of working down in the mines but of working with other men who were dangerous people. "One day I was working with a crew riding on top of a coal train, and this great big fella tried to push me off the train," he told me. "I got so mad and scared, I grabbed him and held on to him, and out of desperation, I bit his neck near the jugular vein. That big fella let me go and never bothered me again. I guess he thought I was crazy."

He soon saved up enough money and headed back to Alabama. "Back in those days there was no safe way to mail or ship money back home to Alabama, so I put most of the money, along with some of my old clothing, in a homemade sack made of three sacks, one inside the other," he said. "And to play it safe, I even put some of my money in the old shoes I was wearing, and some in not-so-secret pockets in the patched overalls I was wearing. Back in those days, I had a lot of money on me." As he finished telling me this story, he took a deep breath and said, "It was by the grace of the good Lord that I made it back to Alabama safe and sound, and bought some land." The land was in Choctaw County, near the Tombigbee River, where the Choctaw and Chickasaw Indians used to roam. It was on this land where he built a house on what we call today our family homestead property.

Shortly thereafter, he married my mother. From this union they had ten children; I was number seven. In spite of being handicapped with rheumatism and arthritis, my father was the hardest-working man I ever laid eyes on. And, needless to say, he made sure that all of us worked hard, too. I didn't like it at the time it was happening, but now when I look back, I can appreciate that it taught me the dignity of labor.

As I look back at all the different business ventures my father had going on almost simultaneously, I am amazed at how he did it, or should I say how we did it. Think about it: my father had a timber logging business that employed several people from outside the family; a farming business; a cattle- and hog-raising business; and a syrup-making business that made sugarcane syrup and sorghum cane molasses. Needless to say, my father was a businessman, and he made sure we were involved in his businesses, and that meant work. I often heard him say, "If you want to be a businessman, you've got to be willing to work hard."

It's funny: every time I heard him say that, I would quietly say to myself, *Is this what being a businessman is like?* I didn't know the answer as a youngster, or perhaps I didn't want to know the answer, but after I grew up and had to enter the world of work, it didn't take me long to answer that rhetorical question: *The answer is yes.*

Although he spent much of his time trying to provide for us, my father made sure we went to school when the work was finished. And he took time out on Sundays and made sure he took us to church. Often I would hear him sing two of his favorite old spirituals: "Shine on Me," and "Lord Help Me on This Journey."

My father was not only a hardworking businessman but a dedicated father and family man. And he was a brave man, one who was not afraid to take chances to be successful.

Finally, I recall a special event that highlights my father's bravery and fortitude. One day he said to me, "Son, I want you to go with me on the log truck and haul a load of logs." I was excited because I enjoyed riding on log trucks. Well, little did I know I was in for the excitement of my life. My father and I drove the truck way up a mountain called Scott Mountain, in the Mount Ararat region in Choctaw County, Alabama.

There was a winding road that went around a section of Scott Mountain. As we traveled the mountain's narrow, winding road, I looked down toward its bottom. I saw what appeared to me as a deep ravine, a seemingly bottomless gulf, covered with kudzu vines and other competing green vegetation.

We finally made it safely around the mountain to the loading site. After the large longleaf-pine logs were finally loaded onto the truck, my father and I got into the truck and began driving slowly around the winding mountain road, curving from left to right. I covered my eyes to keep from gazing down into the deep ravine. My father, sensing that I was scared, slowly stopped the truck and said to me, "Son, I want you to get out of the truck and let me drive alone, so that if something happens, both of us will not die."

I obeyed. My father began slowly driving the truck around the mountain as I followed it at a distance. Suddenly, I noticed the back wheel of the trailer on the right side beginning to rise about six inches off the ground. Upon seeing this, and knowing my father was in the truck, I said one of the shortest prayers one can utter: "Jesus!" The back wheel on the trailer began easing back down to the ground. My father continued driving the truck around the mountain, finally made it to the end of the narrow road, and waited for me.

As I approached, I noticed that he had gotten out of the truck. As he stood in the shadows of surrounding sweet-gum and oak trees, I could see the silhouette of his face, which appeared to have a smile on it. As I drew closer, I noticed that his smile was one of satisfaction as he took a deep breath and breathed a sigh of relief.

Without giving me a chance to tell him what I had seen, he said, "We made it, we made it; thank God we made it!"

I agreed, saying, "Yes, Daddy, we made it; thank God we made it." He didn't know it, but within me, a little voice quietly said, Daddy, *you're a hero.*

There were many others who influenced me in positive ways: the preacher who told me, "Jesus loves you, and with Him you can make it anywhere in the world"; the kind old farmer who always shared with us the fruits of his fields; the teacher who taught us math, even when we were not eager to learn; the cousin who encouraged me to play football when I thought I was too small; and the men and women who went into various branches of the military and served in our wars.

There were many other heroes from every walk of life, big and small, who encouraged me during the foundational stages in my life and do so even now.

One of the greatest highlights in my life came when I graduated from high school at the age of seventeen. My mother had always encouraged me to get an education. Well, to make a long story short, I knew that I had no money to go to college. And my father had told me he wanted me to stay home and become a businessman rather than try to go to college.

I knew, and my mother knew, deep down inside that I had to look for other options to achieve a formal education. It suddenly dawned on me that one of my classmates had a brother who was in the air force and had come home on military leave. Through my classmate, I met him. He was dressed in his blue air force uniform. Man, he was sharp, dressed in that blue air force uniform. I said to him, "I would like to join the air force. Would you tell me how to do it?"

With a smile he said, "Man, air force blue would look good on you; I'll take you to the city to see the recruiter."

He did. I spoke to the recruiter, and after I successfully passed the ASVAB(Armed Service Vocational Aptitude Battery) test, he interviewed me further and discovered I was only seventeen. He gave me an application to fill out and sign. But, he said to me, "Because you're only seventeen, you will need to get one of your parents to sign for you."

Well, needless to say I knew it would be a challenge to get my father to sign for me. However, out of respect for him, I approached him with the application in my hand and said, "Daddy, I want to go into the air force, but because I'm only seventeen, I need you to sign these forms."

"I'm not going to sign them," he said. "I told you before that I want you to stay around here and become a businessman."

My mother overheard the conversation. Later in the evening she took me aside and said to me quietly, "Let's go to the garden alone, just you and me, and yes, bring the application forms with you." We walked and talked in the garden alone. As I gazed into her light brown-gray eyes and noticed the setting sunlight glittering and shimmering through the treetops, dancing on her sandy-red hair, a sense of calmness came over both of us. She beckoned me to hand her the application to go into the air force, and I handed it to her. With tears in her eyes, she signed it.

After that, she said, "I know I'm doing the right thing for you, but there's one thing I want you to remember: don't forget to always pray and ask God to help you."

I had tears in my eyes, too, as I said, "I will, Mama. I will, Mama." We hugged each other. Afterward, we gathered a handful of vegetables from the garden and went back into the house.

Within a few days I had passed the physical exam and was sworn into the US Air Force. Shortly thereafter, I was shipped out to basic training. It was the beginning of a new day and a new journey for me, all because my mother had chosen once again to be a hero in my life.

CHAPTER 2

Searching for Heroes: Looking Without and Looking Within

Remember what was said earlier: People are imitative beings. From the very first day one is born, to the last day here on earth, one is learning to do what one sees and hears others do. In the developmental and foundational stages in our life we have an innate "radar" that enables us to observe other people in action from all walks of life. In this process we learn to select our own heroes, and we invariably try to repeat the actions we see and hear in them to the point of self-ownership. The key to this process is to be able to select our own heroes within our own defined boundaries and parameters.

When you establish these guidelines, you should be able to separate the good heroes from the bad heroes. You must know the difference between a good hero and a so-called bad hero: The good hero is the person who has said something to you or done something for you that prompted you to go forward in a positive way. A bad hero is really not a hero all, because he or she said something to you or did something for you, or to you, that affected you in a negative way. In other words, choose heroes that will build you up rather than tear you down. It is a learning process but a necessary one. It is a process that I have learned throughout my life experience. Remember: experience is a tough teacher and the tuition is costly!

The first stage of searching for heroes in life begins by observing other heroes. The next stage is one of searching for the hero within. The first heroes in the early developmental and foundational stages of my life were undoubtedly my parents and others with whom I had the privilege of coming into contact.

Beginning in my early adolescence, I became increasingly independent, and my contacts in my community expanded. As a consequence, my list of heroes grew longer. During this stage, my heroes included those in movie westerns. The thing that impressed me the most about those movies was the fact that the good guy always won. During my early adolescent years we had access only to a radio. Going to movies, which was rare, was a special privilege. Cowboys such as Tom Mix, Red Ryder, Hopalong Cassidy, Bob Steele, the Lone Ranger and Tonto, and Roy Rogers with Dale Evans were my favorites.

I must have bought every comic book I could get my hands on. (That was really how I first learned to read, seeing the pictures connected to the words.) I loved seeing them in action: shooting their pistols or rifles; roping cattle, horses, and sometimes outlaws; duking it out with the outlaws; mounting, riding, and dismounting their horses. They were my heroes and I was taking it all in. This led me to looking for the hero within myself.

As I watched the cowboys in action in the movies, or read all the available comic books I bought in the local drugstore or traded with other young boys who also loved reading them, I was able to observe over and over again the many ways they would maneuver their pistols or rifles: from the standing position, from the kneeling position, from the prone position, or while riding their horses. I was soaking it all in because I wanted to be like them.

At first, I was not old enough to use real guns, so I made my own wooden pistol or rifle from lumber boards, using an assortment of tools: saws, auger bits, and files from my father's old tool shed.

I practiced mimicking all the moves I saw the cowboys do. I would select any target I could find or imagine. My wooden pistols and rifles could not make sounds, so I created my own: every time I took aim at my target and moved my trigger finger, as if I were pulling a real trigger, I made my own sound: *bang ... bang.* And, in my mind I never missed my target, always thinking positively.

I was ready to graduate to the next level. One year, just before Christmas, someone dressed like Santa Claus came to our house and asked me, as he lifted me into his lap, "Young fella, what would you like to have for Christmas?"

To be truthful, I did not feel comfortable sitting in this unknown Santa Claus's lap. However, without hesitating I answered, "Santa, I would be mighty happy if you would bring me a cap pistol and some candy."

Santa smiled and said, "What else do you want?"

"Santa, I want to get out of your lap now."

He smiled as he said, "I'll put that on my list."

I never did find out who that Santa Claus was. On Christmas Day, I found a large multicolored stocking with my name on it hanging from the Christmas tree. I quickly opened it and found a cap pistol and a package with rolls of caps for shooting it, along with the usual candy, raisins, apples, and oranges. Upon seeing how happy I was to get the cap pistol, my daddy and mama, with smiles on their faces, asked, "Did Santa bring you what you wanted?"

I walked over and hugged them both at the same time as I said, "Yes, sir and yes, ma'am. This has been a good Christmas." Now I had a pistol! Although it could not fire any type of bullets or pellets, it looked like a real gun and could make its own sound, going *pop* every time I pulled the trigger.

Shortly thereafter, I was able to save up enough money to buy a holster for it. Now I was ready to practice with my cap pistol: quick draw from my holster, aim it at the target and shoot, use my trigger finger to spin it around in my hand, and quickly stick it back into my holster—just like I had learned from the "real" cowboys.

One year later, thinking that I was ready to go to the next level of responsibility, I began to tell my father that I wanted to learn more about real weapons. Although he knew I was not ready for real weapons using real bullets, he agreed to ask Santa to bring me a Daisy Red Ryder BB Gun for Christmas. Christmas came, and true to his word, Santa had put one under the Christmas tree wrapped up in Christmas paper with my name on it. Included were several packets of BBs. Each BB measured approximately one-eighth of an inch in diameter.

My father, knowing there would be safety issues in using the BB gun, explained to me that it could be dangerous if not used properly. He reminded me to never shoot at people with it, because it could cause serious injury, especially if you hit someone in the eye. To expand further on the safety issue, he said, "This BB gun is powerful enough to break windows and things, so you be careful with this thing, boy, do you hear me?"

I could tell by the tone of his voice that he was serious. So I respectfully said with a serious and sincere look on my face, "Yes, sir, Daddy, I hear you. I will … I will."

Searching for the Hero Within: The Day I Was Chased by a Water Moccasin

Needless to say, it didn't take me long to go into action with my BB gun. I would practice shooting at cans placed on top of fence posts. I even began making bull's-eye targets to practice on. I practiced and practiced. I played cowboy games with some of the neighborhood boys who also had their own BB guns. We would shoot at each other while ducking and hiding behind trees or buildings. Clearly we were stretching the safety rules. Of course, each one of us had been used to seeing only the "outlaw cowboy" getting hurt. We all had the mind-set that we were "good cowboys"; therefore, we thought we could never be hit. In spite of this attitude, each one of us was hit from time to time. Boys then, like now, thought they were invincible. It's a miracle that none of us was hit in the eye or hurt seriously. It also was a miracle that my father and mother did not know about some of the games we were playing.

It did not take me long to learn that I could kill birds and sometimes rabbits with the BB gun, if I hit them in the right spot. Like the cowboys in the movies, I had learned to hit the intended target.

It was one fall day, sometime in late October, when the oaks, sweet-gum trees, poplars, and other trees indigenous to the South began shedding their leaves. On this particular day, I looked in the closet in the boys' room and quietly removed my BB gun with a bag of extra BBs. I knew that if I was going to be successful hunting snowbirds, my dog could not go with me, so I tied my dog to a leash and headed alone toward a wooded area not far from our house to go bird hunting.

Several times, I had had the fortune of sacking as many as a dozen snowbirds in only one outing. Although the snowbirds were small, they had a lot of meat on them in proportion to their size. I would give them to my mother, and she would clean and cook them for us. They were ever so tasty. That's how it was back in those days: we learned to live by hunting game of all sorts. It was now late in the fall, and I journeyed to the woods and began hunting birds.

It was early evening, and the sun was still peeping over the top of the trees. The soft southern air was beginning to feel slightly crisp and cool. The fresh air mixed with the smell of pines, oak trees, and sweet-gum trees, along with the pervasive aroma of late-autumn wildflowers. It was refreshing, simply walking in the woods. However, my mind was focused on finding those snowbirds.

I walked in the pasture area where the cows normally grazed the green grass that would soon be turning brown. By this time of evening, they had all left the pasture area and made their way to the barn, where they could get extra food. As I walked along the edge of the woods, I followed the often-traveled paths that cows and other animals had made. Finally, after traveling to a lowland area near the creek that ran through our homestead land, I spotted several snowbirds darting from tree to tree and finally perching on a big oak tree limb. I took aim at one of them with my BB gun. I slowly pulled the trigger, and it made the usual noise: *pop*. My aim was right on target, and the bird came tumbling to the ground. I proudly picked it up and placed it in my game bag. As a result of this initial success, I continued my hunt.

For some reason a strange thought came into my mind. I had heard that snakes such as the diamondback rattlesnake and the water moccasin snake are very active during the month of October, as they are looking for food before they go into hibernation. I had been told that a bite from either one of those snakes could be deadly, especially if you were alone and could not get medical help right away. Suddenly, I realized I had to add another dimension to my bird hunting. I began paying closer attention to where I was walking while at the same time looking up into the trees, hoping to spot a treasured snowbird.

For some strange reason I could not get that "snake thought" out of my mind. Suddenly, I heard a shuffling sound. It didn't sound like a four-legged creature that made a skipping sound as it walked. Neither did it sound like a rattlesnake, which often makes a rattling sound with its tail area when feeling threatened. Rather, it was an incessant sound as if something was sliding through the fallen leaves and green grass. The sound got louder and louder.

Suddenly I turned around, and as I was turning, I saw what looked like a water moccasin coming toward me with its head raised off the ground, its mouth wide open. Instantly I dropped onto one knee with my rifle in shooting position, just like I had learned from the cowboys. I aimed at the snake's mouth, which was wide open and coming straight at me. Instinctively, I fired the BB gun. The snake instantly dropped his head, veered to my right, crawled up into a small pine tree, and hung from it, motionless. To make sure the snake was dead, I fired several more shots into its head. It remained motionless, hanging over the tree limb. I waited for a while to make sure it was dead: it was dead all right! Still shaking, I quietly said to myself, *Thank God for cowboys and guardian angels.* I have told this true story over the years to others. No one was ever convinced this really happened.

Searching for the Hero Within: Roping the Wild Bull That No One Else Could Catch

I had the privilege of being raised on a family-owned farm, which meant we always had cattle, horses, hogs, and pigs, as well as an assortment of other animals. As soon as I was big enough to climb up onto a horse or mule, I began learning how to ride them, just like the cowboys in the movies. I began learning to use a rope to lasso standing objects such as fence posts and cows from a standing position. I soon graduated to the next level by lassoing running cows as I was riding on a horse. It was a fun thing to do. I practiced hour after hour and got better and better. I even felt that I was as good as the cowboys in the movies.

I got good at roping and lassoing animals—so much so that I became an asset to my father's business in that I could rope cattle, hogs, and pigs. He recognized my skill. I was now thirteen years old, going on fourteen. He heard of a cattle farmer who had a wild bull that no one could catch, including the farmer. He contacted the farmer and arranged to take me to his cattle farm.

After the usual greeting, my father said to the cattle farmer, "This is my boy. I believe he can rope the wild bull that no one can catch."

The farmer looked me up and down and began laughing. Then with a scowl on his face, he said, "This boy is too little to rope a bull!" Then he paused, and after scratching his head for a while, he asked me, "Are you sure you want to try it?"

After almost saying no, I said, "I'm willing to give it a try." He and Daddy agreed that we would return the next day. He reminded us that he needed time to round up a few men to drive the bull out into the open.

That night was a sleepless one for me. I tossed and turned most of the night as I pondered how to rope that wild bull. Finally, morning came, and several of my brothers and sisters and I, along with Daddy, gathered at the round table for breakfast. My mother remained in the kitchen along with some of my sisters.

As we ate breakfast that morning, we all watched Daddy go through his usual ritual of drinking coffee. He had a unique habit of drinking coffee from the saucer: he poured the steaming coffee from the cup into the saucer, blew into the saucer to cool it somewhat, and then drank it with a slurping sound that resonated throughout the house.

I noticed that he had a faraway look on his face that day, and he was strangely silent about his agenda for us. Suddenly, it entered my mind that Daddy had not told Mama or my brothers and sisters that he and I were going to try to catch a wild bull on the cattle farmer's place that day. Sensing that, I remained mum about it, too.

Suddenly, Daddy rose from the breakfast table and told the rest of the family as he said, pointing toward me, "You and I are going to take a trip just to the other side of Butler; we'll be back shortly." No one questioned Daddy. That's the way it was in those days.

On that late spring day, I rushed into the room where the boys slept, quickly put on my boots and cowboy hat, and checked in the back of the truck to make sure my old faithful lassoing rope was there. Daddy and I, without saying much to each other, drove to the other side of Butler, about seven miles from our house. Upon arriving at the dirt road leading to the cattle farmer's house, we made a right turn and continued driving. The old dirt road was lined with tall southern pines, huge red oak trees, sweet-gum trees, and magnolias; nestled beneath were black-eyed Susans mingled in with other green vegetation. It was still morning. I could smell the fragrance in the soft southern air mixed with the evaporating dewdrops, and the dominant smell of pines and sweet gums competing with the fragrance of the wildflowers.

Upon arriving at the cattle farmer's house, we found that he was waiting for us. He told us he had decided on the best location to position me for the possibility of roping the wild bull. He said to my father, "I want you to stay here while I take your boy and station him alone, at a place where he will not be easily noticed." As the cattle farmer and I left Daddy at the farmhouse, I looked back over my shoulder: I could see him standing there, nodding with a sign of affirmation, yet seemingly with a nervous smile.

The cattle farmer led me into an open area where we traveled along a foot-trodden, sun-baked clay path. Clearly it was an old pathway that had been frequently used by humans and animals. He led me to a side fence that faced an open grass field between the fence and a wooded area. Finally he led me along the fence to an area that had a recessed space with a gate to one of the corner posts made from old creosote-treated railroad tires.

The old cattle farmer suggested I stand behind the post in the recessed area. Upon further discussion he and I agreed this was a good location. He reminded me that he was going to have the men he was using as "drivers" try to run the wild bull from the wooded area toward the fence leading to me. I knew what he meant by "drivers" because that was how we often hunted deer:

we would station hunters at strategic hunting stations and use the "drivers" to run the deer in their direction. I said to him, "That's similar to what we do when deer hunting."

He nodded and said, "Little fellow, you've got the picture." Then he said, "Now, I am going to get the boys to enter the wooded area and attempt to drive the bull out into the opening and hopefully in your direction." As he walked away, he glanced back over his shoulder with a curious smile on his face and said, "Good luck."

I tied one end of the rope to the post I was to stand behind. My prior experience had taught me that I could not hold a bull that weighed more than seven hundred pounds going at a speed of some thirty miles per hour.

As I stood there waiting, I noticed on that late spring morning that the invigorating air smelled as fresh as ever as the southern breeze blew softly in my face. My heart began beating faster as I anticipated what to do if the wild bull came running my way. To be honest, my first thought was to run! But I soon collected myself by thinking in a more positive way: remembering what I had learned about roping and the success I had had before, I said to myself, *I can do it, I can do it.* Shortly thereafter, a calmness came over me as if "angels unaware" were watching over me saying, "We are with you, and we will not let you fail."

Suddenly, I heard an old familiar sound coming from the wooded area. It was the bull drivers making noise: "Wooo, wooo, wooo ..." Shortly thereafter, I heard a rustling sound coming from the wooded area. At first I could not see what it was because it was too far away. But I could faintly hear a snorting sound. It sounded like the bull! The snorting sound began getting louder and louder, and now I could see that it was a huge brownish-red bull with long horns, heading toward the fence. It made a left turn at the fence and headed in my direction. As he headed in my direction, going faster and faster, I could hear the hoofbeats sounding *clickety-clack ... clickety-clack.*

17

I said to myself, *This is my moment to do what I was taught to do: Grip the lasso [the loop] part of the rope properly in my right hand while holding the circle-lapped parts properly in my left hand. Focus on the proper timing of the swirling. Focus on the proper projectile. And focus on the proper release action. It's a matter of practicing and practicing until you reach the point of overlearning.* Well, I was ready.

Now the moment of truth was getting closer and closer. It was like a dream as the wild bull came charging next to the fence near me. The wind must have been blowing in the direction he was heading, because it appeared he did not smell me. A bull or cow is a lot like a deer: they have a keen sense of smell. Nevertheless, he kept running next to the fence. Just at the right moment, as he was getting ready to pass me, I could see his great big horns. With a quick swirling motion of the lasso, I released it, and with a perfect loop, it caught the wild bull by the horns. The bull, with the thrust of his weight and speed, flipped in midair, landed on the ground, and just lay there, almost motionless.

I looked up and saw the farmer and Daddy running toward us. The old farmer was leading the way. When he saw what had happened—I had caught the wild bull that no one else had been able to catch—he yelled, "By George, he did it! By George, he did it!" with a look of glee on his face.

Daddy came right behind him, leaping above the ground as if walking on air. Finally he fell to the ground and began rolling on it, saying, in a loud voice, "I told you so! I told you so!"

The men who were helping the farmer rushed over to the bull, which was still lying on the ground as if playing possum. The men quickly put another rope over the bull's horns and a second rope around its waist. The farmer and Daddy walked over to me and hugged me as the farmer said, "Boy, you're some kind of cowboy! I been around a long time, but I never seen anyone do what you did."

And Daddy, after hearing what the old farmer said, replied, "I told you so. I told you so!"

The farmer patted me on the shoulder and said, "I am so thankful for what you did. I know your daddy is mighty proud of you."

My father responded by putting his arms around me as he looked in the old farmer's direction, saying, "This is my boy ... This is my boy."

I said to the farmer, "Thanks for letting me be the best cowboy I can."

Searching for the Hero Within: Catching a Greasy Pig in the Greasy Pig Contest.

Part of my father's farming business was raising pigs and hogs for sale. People would come from all around to buy pigs from us. My father had taught me how to catch a pig. He taught me how to corner the pig and then, with one motion, sweep it off its feet. "After you sweep him off his feet, you scoop him up in your arms and hold him with his feet pointing away from you, and pull him close to your chest with your arms and hands interlocked." My father was a good teacher, and I was a good listener. It was a fun game, catching pigs. I practiced and practiced until it became second nature to me. By now, I had gotten used to getting in the "muck and mire" catching pigs. It was a dirty task, but it was fun. And of course I became an asset to my father's business in catching pigs for people who wanted to buy them.

One day my father heard that a country fair sponsored by the state Department of Agriculture was coming to a town in Choctaw County and that one of the activities would be a greasy pig contest. He told me there would be two categories, one for ages ten to fourteen, and one for ages sixteen to eighteen. The winner would get a prize plus be able to keep the pig. I was fourteen at the time and without a doubt had caught many pigs. I had not had an occasion to catch a greasy pig, but I had caught many muddy pigs after they had been soaking and wallowing in the muddy pigsty with its muck and mire.

My father encouraged me to enter the contest. He said, "I believe you could catch one of those greasy pigs if you simply do what you've learned to do: sweep the pig off its feet, scoop it up in your arms, pull it to your chest with its feet pointing away from you, and hold it with your arms and hands interlocked."

I responded to his encouragement, "Daddy, let's go to this fair. I want to enter the greasy pig contest."

Shortly thereafter, we headed for the country fair. People from all around were there. There was a lot of excitement to be had: bull riding and a roping contest, to name a few activities, plus all kinds of exhibits and games. And all you could eat of barbecue, fruit, nuts, and candies. Of course the cotton candy was my favorite.

In the midst of all the fun, I almost forgot the main reason I had come to the fair. Suddenly I remembered: the greasy pig contest. An announcer went through the crowd calling out the time and location of each major event. At first I did not pay much attention to him, but then I heard him yell, "Get ready for the greasy pig contest, folks. It'll be in a specially made pigpen in the back. All contestants are to report immediately." Daddy and I hurried to the announced location. The crowd of spectators had already begun to gather around the specially made pigpen.

It was clear that the sponsors of the greasy pig contest had gone to great lengths to make sure catching the pig would be difficult. The pen was fenced in with special lumber made from rough sawed oak. It was rectangular in shape, about forty feet by thirty feet. The ground within it was a mixture of a thin layer of grass grown on a thin layer of topsoil over clay that was soaked with water.

Several greasy pigs had been placed in the pen earlier in the day, along with extra water and food. By now, the pigs had turned the entire pen's surface into mostly mud, mixed with the usual sty muck and mire. The odor was very familiar: it smelled like a pigpen. It was clear by now that between the greasy pig soaked with motor oil and the mud mixed with muck, it would be quite a challenge for both the pig and the contestants to stay on their feet.

It was time for the contest. The person in charge called on the handlers to remove all pigs from the pig pen except one which was placed in a cage. The person in charge instructed all contestants to get ready. "Boys, the contest is simple: you will be placed along the four fences in the pen, the pig will be located in the middle of the pen, and when you hear me blow the whistle, you are to see if you can catch the greasy pig. The one who catches the pig first will be the winner."

He instructed the handlers to bring one pig in a small cage and set it in the middle of the pen. With a loud yell he said to the contestants, "Line up, boys, on the inside of the pen, along the four walls. And when I blow the whistle, the contest is on." Next he instructed the handlers to open the cage and release the pig in the middle of the pen. The referee blew the whistle. The contest was on!

The five contestants, including me, immediately went chasing after the pig, slipping and sliding on the muddy surface. The pig was also slipping and sliding in the mud as it tried to escape our grasps. Some of the boys were falling on their faces as they lunged at the pig. Mud was flying everywhere. It didn't take us long to realize that the initial challenge was to stay on our feet.

With the mud flying in all directions, most of us were almost immediately bathed in it: muddy clothes, muddy faces, and muddy hands. That was fun in itself. One of the boys was somewhat fat and probably thought that if he could dive onto the pig, he could smother him with his weight. He dived onto the pig, but the pig escaped, with mud flying. Some of the other boys tried catching the pig by the legs but could not hold it. The pig slipped from their grasp because of the grease, along with the other slippery muck and mire.

21

By now I had discovered a pattern in the pig's behavior: it always seemed to go toward the corners of the pen, perhaps thinking that was its best chance of escape. With this in mind, I thought about what I had been taught by my father and what I knew through experience.

Finally, after many failed attempts by the other contestants to catch the pig, it headed toward the corner I was standing near. As he skidded to the corner, I swept him off his feet, scooped him up in my arms, and pulled him to my chest just as I had been taught. Immediately, my father, with the permission of the referee, brought a croker sack to the gate for me to put the pig in. The treasured pig was safely and securely tied up in my sack. Needless to say, I was bubbling over with excitement as the crowd cheered.

The judge announced me the winner of the greasy pig contest. As I smiled and attempted to wipe away some of the mud and muck from my face, the crowd applauded me and someone said, "Atta boy, young man, that's the way to go git 'um."

Needless to say, my father was the happiest one in the whole crowd. After the other awards were given to me, he and I took the pig home.

I named him Winner. He was my favorite pet. I took charge of feeding him myself. Winner became one of the fattest pigs on our farm. It's strange but true that every time I looked at Winner, I was reminded of how many heroes we have in life if we search for them. And they are the ones who help us find the hero within ourselves.

CHAPTER 3

Expanding the Search for Heroes: Training and Serving as an Air Policman in the US Air Force

Upon entering the military in 1955, I realized how much I was indebted to my mother, who signed for me to go into the US Air Force at the tender age of seventeen. She had always wanted me to go to college, and she and I fully understood that joining the US Air Force was a means toward that end while serving my country for at least four years.

I had already made up my mind to have the military payroll department transfer part of my paycheck to a designated bank account. Without a doubt, this was a major crossroads in my life: it was the beginning of a new journey and one that, more and more, required me to grow up fast.

After spending twelve weeks in basic training in Texas, I was given orders to report to an air base in Albuquerque, New Mexico, to be assigned to the Air Police Squadron. This was the beginning of my training as a military policeman. Upon my arrival on base, I was assigned to an air police training school for about two weeks, where I was taught the basics of the military code of justice, self-defense techniques, how to fire and maintain military weapons that were used by military policemen, and the weapons' safety procedures. We were the fighting men of the US Air Force, so to speak. Our job was to provide security for the entire base and enforce military law and order. After my two weeks of training I was assigned to work several weeks with a senior air policeman. And after I was evaluated, I was on my own.

It didn't take me long to realize that this was for real. The base-gate duty was the best because I got to dress up in my class-A uniform while wearing a white web belt to which a loaded 45-caliber pistol in a holster was attached on my right side and a billy club was attached on my left. However, most often I was assigned security duty, which required me to wear the combat fatigue uniform and carry an M-1 rifle while walking around a tall barbed-wire fence that secured the base radar site where airmen were monitoring the skies night and day. It was an eight-hour shift.

One night I was assigned to the midnight shift, from 11:00 p.m. to 7:00 a.m. I was dressed in the usual fatigue uniform armed with a loaded M-1 rifle. The midnight shift was a lonely shift: I was out there all alone. During those long hours I had a long time to think about and reflect on things. On this particular night I began to think about the magnitude and far-reaching value of our military. Our men and women were serving somewhere around the world twenty-four hours a day, on the sea, in the air, and on land. I reflected on the many heroes who served in the military. All made sacrifices in some capacity, and some paid the supreme sacrifice by giving their life in serving our country, America. Although many go unrecognized, these men and women represent some of our finest heroes.

Many of you, like me, have relatives who have served or are serving our country in the military. As I was reflecting on these thoughts, it suddenly dawned upon me that I was part of this elite group, the military armed forces.

I recalled when I was sworn into the US Air Force, I was required to repeat the US Armed Forces Oath of Enlistment: "I, [state name of enlistee], do solemnly swear [or affirm] that I will support and defend the Constitution of the United States against all enemies, foreign and domestic; that I will bear true faith and allegiance to the same; and that I will obey the orders of the President of the United States and the orders of the officers appointed over me, according to regulations and the Uniform Code of Military Justice. So help me God" *(www.Militaryspot. com/air-force/)*. I said to myself, *This is serious business.*

The US Air Forces attracted men and women from all over the United States as well as from other countries. It afforded me the opportunity to mingle with men and women from many different states in America, as well as from other countries. It was a great learning environment, and one that required you to grow up fast. I was ready and willing to go and grow. Many of my fellow airmen had served tours overseas, and as I talked with them, my desire to go overseas grew stronger and stronger.

Soon I found that my dream was about to come true: one day as I was going through my mail, I found an air force letter with orders saying I was being transferred to Okinawa, Japan. I packed my duffel bag and other luggage and headed back to Alabama for a thirty-day leave before reporting to San Francisco to board a ship for Okinawa.

Upon arriving at an air force base in San Francisco, I was assigned to the housing area where the military personnel stayed while waiting for deployment. I was told that I would be held over for two weeks waiting for a military-and-dependents transport ship to arrive. After hearing this news, I said to myself, *I'll have a lot of free time to go sightseeing!*

The next day I discovered that the duty officer had other ideas: he gathered all who were awaiting deployment and gave us job assignments. Well, to make a long story short, I had KP duty for about six hours each day. Nevertheless, I had the opportunity to go sightseeing. I discovered that San Francisco is a beautiful city on the shores of the Pacific Ocean with its mighty Golden Gate Bridge and its cable cars. In addition, I had an opportunity to visit the USO facility in Oakland.

In spite of KP duty, time went by fast. The officer in charge called all who were waiting to be deployed to tell us that our ship had come to shore. "You are to be packed and ready to board ship tomorrow morning at 0900," he said. "Remember, you can only take a duffel bag and one additional bag, nothing more."

The next morning we boarded the ship and were assigned to the lower part, near the engine room. We all were excited and full of anticipation. The ship left shore and headed out to sea. By this time many of us had come to the upper deck to gaze upon the shoreline of San Francisco. It was a breathtaking experience. The seagulls darted all around us as they casually flew in the air, which smelled like seawater.

A funny thing soon happened: as the ship sailed under the Golden Gate Bridge, some of the soldiers, marines, and airmen were already hanging their heads over the railings. They were seasick already, making a nonmelodious sound: "ugh … ugh." The sailors assigned to the ship thought it was funny. I did too.

As we sailed from the shores of San Francisco, the land began to disappear from sight as the ship moved farther into the Pacific Ocean. Soon all we could see was an endless body of water. It was as if I was going to the end of the world. When night came, I was astonished at how many stars—even clusters of stars—I could see in the sky. It caused me to revisit a question I had asked many times before: who created it all? And as usual, a little voice within me answered, "Somebody bigger than you and me."

It was time for the troops in my group to retire for the night. Each one of us was assigned to a canvas-type bunk bed that swayed to and fro, making rhythmic squeaking sounds as the ship sailed through the rough waves. The engines in the boiler room nearby would always let us know when they came under extra stress caused by encountering rough waters. It would cause the engines to rev up as it made a soon-familiar, special humming sound. At first the sound was annoying, but we quickly got used to it.

We were told that we were going to make a stop in Hawaii and then sail to Formosa (today it is called Taiwan). From there we would sail to Okinawa. When I heard this news, I became excited and full of anticipation again. I said to myself, *One of the benefits of being in the military is that you get to travel free, and you have the opportunity to see many places in the world.*

Upon arriving in Hawaii, the officer in charge told those of us who were being deployed that we had to stay on the ship when it docked. Only the assigned sailors, officers, and dignitaries would be allowed to disembark. To us, this was a letdown. Suddenly, it dawned on me: I'm in the military now. I do what I'm told.

At night we would often gather on the upper deck and look up into the skies with darkness all around us. As I gazed up and looked at all the stars and star clusters, I said to myself, What a beautiful sight!

Although at this stage in my life, I did not read the Bible on a regular basis—and when I did, I did not understand it—I always kept one of those little pocket Bibles issued to us in the military in my possession. On this night I recalled having read in Isaiah 40:26 NIV: "Lift your eyes to the heavens: Who created all these? He who brings out the starry host one by one, and calls them each by name." As I pondered the question of who had created all these stars and much more, I said to myself, *Surely it was not mere man. Only God could do all this!*

Soon the ship set sail toward Formosa. Day and night there was no land to be seen. Seeing all this water as far as my eyes could see, I was reminded that as a young child in Sunday school I had read in Genesis 1 NIV, "In the beginning God created the heavens and the earth ... then God said, 'Let the waters below the heavens be gathered into one place, and let the dry land appear':

and it was so … God called the dry land earth, and the gathering of the waters He called seas, and God saw that it was Good." And then I reflected on what I had learned in school—that according to scientists, about 71 percent of the earth's surface is covered by water (68 percent salt water, 3 percent freshwater); only about 29 percent is covered by land. Now that I was out in middle of all this water, I questioned God: "Lord, why so much water?"

Somewhere between Hawaii and Formosa (Taiwan) I found out how it feels to be seasick. I recalled having made fun of my fellow airmen who had gotten seasick while the ship was sailing under the Golden Gate Bridge. It was their turn to laugh at me. It happened one day while we were sitting at the dining hall table with food in our individual trays. Suddenly, the ship entered rough waters and began reeling and rocking. I recall that as I was eating, I looked up from my tray momentarily and then back down again. It was then that I discovered that my tray was sliding toward the end of the table and back toward me as the ship swayed right to left … right to left. Soon my mind began to lose its equilibrium, resulting in my becoming nauseated. Simply put, I was seasick. If you have never been seasick, trust me, it is one of the worst feelings I have ever had. Every time I thought about eating food, especially greasy food, I became more seasick and headed for the nearest latrine with the usual sound: "ugh … ugh." It was a humbling experience that had me asking myself, *Where is the hero in you now?* As strange as it sounds, the only kind of food I could eat to settle my stomach was sardines. Can you imagine that? Way out in the middle of the Pacific Ocean, wanting sardines. Thank God for sardines!

A few days passed and we arrived in Formosa. Again, those of us who were slated to go to Okinawa could not leave the ship. After a few hours, the ship set sail for Okinawa. Incidentally, I had just about recovered from my seasickness. I could not wait to step on dry land. Good news: we were told that we would be arriving on the shores of Okinawa within hours. We were told to have all our belongings—one duffel bag and one tote bag—and be ready to disembark from the ship. I was ready to see dry land again. We had now been on this ship, at sea, about nineteen days.

Our ship finally arrived on the shores of Okinawa. As I gazed upon its shoreline, I could see that it was a beautiful island with beautiful white sand beaches, tall palm trees swayed with the trade winds, and green grass, even in mid-February.

As we were disembarking, I noticed that the airmen who had served their eighteen months on Okinawa were getting ready to board the ship to return to the United States. You could tell they were seasoned veterans by now.

As I stepped onto dry land, loaded down with my duffel and tote bag, I began what I thought would be routine walking, but I soon discovered that it felt as if the ground was constantly moving beneath my feet. The other airmen in my group felt the same way. Someone said, "This is how it is when you have been sailing in a ship, especially for nineteen days." Soon, we climbed into the waiting four-by-four vehicles and were transported to the air base, where we were processed. I was excited and filled with anticipation. I said to myself, *So this is Okinawa.* Remember, I had just turned nineteen.

After going through the processing stages, we were briefed on some of the unique culture and customs that we would be exposed to, and how we were to act in the process of becoming acclimated to our new environment. Next, we air policemen were taken to our special barracks. The sergeant on duty assigned us to our respective barracks and bunk areas.

On our very first assignment the next day we began a two-day training session designed to familiarize us with the types of weapons, ammunition, uniforms, military code of laws, and other related information required for our special duties.

Our duties as air policemen were essentially the same as they had been stateside: security patrol, base patrol, base-gate duty, aircraft protection on the flight line guard duty, and directing

29

traffic on special occasions. On our time off, we were allowed to go off base and enjoy the amenities available in the various villages and small towns. The military, no matter what branch, had a standing rule: you could essentially do what you wanted, as long as you stayed out of trouble and reported for your assigned duty on time. It didn't take long for most of us to adapt to the everyday routine.

One day a sergeant noticed that I was going downtown on R and R with other airmen who were described as a "rough bunch." He took me under his wings, so to speak. "Airman, I advise you to stick close to my side," he said to me. "That way I can keep you out of trouble."

It did not take me long to realize that this sergeant was looking out for my well-being. In fact, this same sergeant noticed an announcement on a bulletin board asking for volunteers in our air police squadron to sign up for special duty with the armed forces police headquarters on an army base. He was familiar with the job and told me that those who signed up would be stationed on an army base and perform duty alongside combined military personnel from the army, the marines, and the navy, as well as other airmen. We would be assigned to either foot patrol or highway patrol. Sarge looked at me and said, "I'm going to sign up for this duty." Sarge was about six feet, three inches tall, and weighed at least a solid 200 pounds. I was about five feet, seven inches and weighed about 150 pounds soaking wet. Suddenly, Sarge looked at me and asked, "Why don't you sign up, too?"

"Now, Sarge, you know I am too small for that kind of duty," I replied.

He looked at me with a reassuring smile and said, "Little fellow, you're one tough dude. Besides, I'll look out for you. Let's go sign up!"

Hesitantly, I said, "Okay. If you say so, I'll sign up."

We both signed up, and within a few days we were shipped to the army base and assigned to the armed forces police unit. Clearly, this was another major turning point in my life. As I reflected on how I ended up in the armed forces police, I concluded that it was because this sergeant was a hero in my life, for he had encouraged me to go forward.

After arriving on the army base, we were assigned our living quarters so that we could unpack our usual duffel bag and tote bag.

The sergeant in charge was ready to assign us to the town patrol unit or the highway patrol unit and began sizing us up. He looked at my friend Sarge and with a smile of satisfaction told him, "Sergeant, I am going to assign you to the town patrol group." Then he looked at me with what seemed to be a condescending smile and said, "I am going to assign you to the highway patrol unit." Sarge looked at me and smiled, and gave me a thumbs-up sign.

Well, it didn't take me long to realize that the highway patrolmen were more involved than I had envisioned. Fortunately, I already had both a military and a civilian driver's license. I had to go through a one-week orientation training to learn how to operate the patrol car radiophone, how to read the maps of Okinawa, how to write traffic tickets, how to investigate traffic accidents, and how to respond to emergency calls in various Okinawan towns to aid the town patrol sub-units. It was a lot to digest in one week, but I passed the test.

Now I was ready to ride on highway patrol with an experienced partner. At first, my job was to operate the radio—to send and receive calls. After only one month, I was assigned to drive one of the patrol cars. Sometimes my partner would be a sailor; other times it could be an army soldier, a marine, or another airman like me. On many occasions, my partner was an Okinawan native who was a civilian police officer. I soon discovered that one of the Okinawan policemen who often rode as my partner owned a judo *dojo* (school). He regularly invited me to attend, but at first, I did not accept his invitation. To be frank, I did not know what judo was.

As fate would have it, it didn't take me long to find out. Remember: in my stateside training in air police school I had been taught basic self-defense. Well, I soon found out that the little self-defense I had been taught was not sufficient for dealing with the rough GIs frequenting the various off-base towns and villages.

One night I was assigned to patrol duty on the night shift. I was scheduled to drive the patrol car, and my army partner rode in the passenger seat, manning the radio. Normally, on night shift we patrolled the many highways on Okinawa as well as the towns, coordinating with the town patrol unit and assisting them whenever needed.

Suddenly, the police dispatcher's voice came over the radio, asking for the location of all cable cars. Each patrol car had a cable car number. I was driving cable one. We could hear the urgency in his voice as the dispatcher asked cable one for its location. My partner answered by telling him we were near the town of Old Village. The dispatcher said, "The town patrol policeman in Old Village is reporting a big fight between some marines and some sailors. They need help! Report immediately and assist. I will send other reinforcements as soon as I can locate them."

My partner answered with the usual code number: "Ten-four" (meaning "okay"). We sped off to Old Village and drove along the main street. It was lined with many bars and hangouts for GIs.

In front of one of the bars, we spotted one of the town patrol soldiers waving for us to stop and help them. My partner and I hurriedly parked our patrol car and rushed to the bar, where I saw my friend Sarge, who was one of the town patrol soldiers assigned to Old Village that night. He said, "There were several marines and sailors fighting inside the bar. We got most of them to stop with the exception of three or four." Then he said, "You fellas on patrol duty will probably have to take some of these guys back to their bases and turn them over to the sergeant on duty." Of course by now Sarge had recognized me. He said to us, "Let's get inside and take care of business."

By now, several other patrol cars had arrived on the scene. As we entered the bar where the GIs were fighting, it became clear to me that most of them had had too much to drink. Fortunately, no one was seriously hurt, but they basically had torn up the place: broken tables were turned over, and shattered chairs were scattered all around. The Okinawan owners of the bar were standing at a safe distance, peeping from behind the bar with a look of despair. We assured them that everything would be all right and that we would report the damage to the proper military authority. Upon hearing this they gave us the customary Japanese response and said, *"Arigato"* (thank you).

It appeared by now that everything had settled down somewhat. At least we thought so. Several of the marines as well as several sailors had been told that we were going to take them back to their respective bases. Most of them accepted our orders. However, one marine, a big muscular fellow, said he was not going anywhere. I walked toward him and said, "Let's go to the patrol car. We're going to take you back to your base."

This marine looked at me, dressed in my air force blue uniform, wearing my billy club on my left side and my 45-caliber pistol on my right, and said, "Ain't no fly boy going to arrest me," and came charging after me like a wild bull. As he lunged at me, I tried to grab control of him, but his weight and momentum caused both of us to go tumbling over a broken table. As I looked up, I saw my friend Sarge grab this marine, pick him up, and body-slam him to the floor, facedown. We immediately handcuffed the drunk marine and took him to the patrol car with one of his buddies who would escort him back to his base with us and turn him over to the sergeant in charge. Before driving away, my friend Sarge looked at me and said, "I told you I've got your back."

"Thanks, Sarge," I said. "I owe you one."

As we were driving the marines back to their base, we began talking with the drunk man's buddy who was accompanying him. He apologized for causing all the trouble back in town. He then mentioned that he and his buddy along with their battalion had just come off a two-week combat training mission way out in the "boonies." He went on to say, "That training makes us mean and wanna fight somebody."

I said, "We understand, but you've got to learn when to stop."

My partner added, "You guys have got to remember, some of these sailors have been at sea a long time, and when they come ashore, they can be pretty mean too."

The marine buddy sitting in the backseat, said, "You're making a good point, but you know us marines: we ain't gonna let nobody beat us."

Upon arriving at the marine base, we reminded the buddy that we were going to turn them over to the sergeant on duty. "Here's what we want you to do: Take the drunk marine and put him in the shower, and then take him to his bunk. Make sure that neither of you come back to the village tonight. You got that, marine?"

"Yes, sir. We thank you for looking out for us."

We removed the handcuffs from the drunk marine and turned him over to the sergeant on duty. I whispered in the sergeant's ear, "We will not file any individual charges. Just make sure these two marines don't go back into town tonight."

The sergeant on duty winked at us and said, "I read you ... I read you."

Now that things were back to normal, I reflected on the fact that we as members of the US Armed Forces—airmen, soldiers, marines, and sailors—were all part of the same mission. Therefore, we needed to always look out for one another. I could have easily written the drunk marine up and charged him and perhaps caused him to be court-martialed. But we didn't in this case or in other cases such as this unless absolutely necessary. I said to myself, *It's the right thing to do. We, the armed forces, are in this together and must look out for each other.*

Several days after this encounter it was my turn to work on the day shift. The Okinawan civilian police force would often assign one of their policemen to ride with us. A wonderful coincidence happened on my day shift: the Okinawan officer who had been assigned to ride with me several times before was assigned to ride with me again. He was the one who had invited me to come to his judo school (dojo) several times before.

On that particular day as we were patrolling the highways and roadways, I noticed he had a big smile on his face. "We heard the news that you got roughed up a few nights ago in Old Village," he said. "Are you okay now?"

"Yes, sir, I'm okay," I replied.

He took the opportunity to mention that his school taught self-defense as well as sport judo. "Would you visit my school tomorrow evening?" he asked.

For some strange reason I was ready to say yes, and I answered, "Yes, sir, I'll be there." I didn't know it at the moment, but that was the beginning toward another major milestone in my life.

The next day, at approximately 5:00 p.m., I arrived at the location where my future *sensei* (judo teacher) had directed me. As I drove along a dirt road that was well kept, with beautiful palm trees and neatly manicured green lawns, and dotted with small homes, I noticed a rectangular building on the left with a sign on the front. I could not read the Japanese writing on it, but below that, it said "Ping Pong Hall." I continued driving along the dirt road with several Okinawan homes on both sides. I soon noticed a large rectangular building that had several equally spaced windows along its walls.

As I drove closer, I could see a large sign above the entrance with Japanese writing on it, and beneath it *"Judo Dojo"* (judo school). My sensei, whom I found out later owned the school, saw me approaching the dojo. He quickly opened the door and came out and greeted me, and after he directed me to park in the special parking area on the side, he escorted me into the building. As we entered, I noticed that several students nearby gave him the traditional Japanese standing salutation: they bowed to him. He directed one of his senior students to continue leading the class in *taiso* (calisthenics) until he returned.

He then took me to his office and invited me to kneel on one side of a typical low table, Japanese-style, as he did likewise on the other side, directly across from me. He said with a reassuring smile, "Welcome to my judo dojo. I am so happy you finally came."

I nervously answered, "Sir, I thank you for inviting me."

He went on to say, "Judo is good for self-defense, and sport, and it is good for your mind and body. You will learn much if you work hard. We practice every evening from 5:00 p.m. to 7:00 p.m. To practice judo you must learn many rules."

After that, he escorted me around his office and showed me one of his pictures on the wall, and a picture framed with his judo certification. Upon looking at his certification, I noticed that he held the rank of Rokudan (sixth degree black belt, which I found out later after learning more about judo). He also showed me pictures of some of his former students, some of whom were American GIs. Then he reminded me that that night, my first session, he would introduce me to his class, and afterward I would sit and observe them as they practiced.

After being introduced, I sat and observed him taking his class through successive stages of practice: (1) *taiso* (calisthenics—warming up and limbering the body), (2) *ukemi* (falling exercise), (3) *kata* (prearranged methods of practicing techniques), (4) *uchikomi* (an exercise for practicing form development—the correct action of your body in applying the technique), and (5) *randori* (free technique exercise whereby the actual application of the technique is practiced against a partner who is defending himself or trying to throw you).

His was a typical Japanese class, one that was regimented and emphasized practicing the basic skills with a lot of repetition—no shortcuts. Even today, I appreciate this method of teaching.

While watching them practice, I noticed there were other American GIs in his class. I soon learned that most of them were marines. What stood out on this first night was the falling techniques: forward falling, side falling, backward falling, tumbling falling, and throwing each other. They would break their falls by slapping against the *tatami* (straw) mats with a loud sound: *bam … bam.*

I got dizzy simply from watching. The class ended at 7:00 p.m. My sensei walked me to the door with a great big smile on his face and said, "I'll see you tomorrow."

I replied, "Yes, sir. I'll see you tomorrow."

It was the beginning of months of training in the art of judo and self-defense classes, sometimes seven days a week, including participating in tournaments throughout the island of Okinawa.

On the second day I reported to the dojo for classes, my sensei fitted me with a *judo-gi* (judo uniform) and showed me how to tie the traditional white belt for beginners over the jacket around the waist area. He then told me that the first technique one must learn in judo is falling. It is not safe to practice judo unless you learn how to fall. On the first day of practice one of his senior students was assigned to teach me how to fall properly: backward, forward, to the side, and tumbling.

I was assigned to this routine for two classes. The senior student, upon being satisfied with my falling techniques, then took me through the next stage by throwing me to the mat over and over again, testing my ability to fall. Each time he threw me, he could tell whether or not I was breaking my falls properly by listening to the sound of my hand and upper arm slapping against the mat: *bam … bam.* Repetition: over and over again.

At first, it was a dizzying experience. Day by day, falling became second nature to me because it was part of our daily routine in judo, as part of our routine exercises.

As I became more acclimated to the system of practicing the techniques, I found out how much there was to learn: *tachiwaza* (throwing techniques), *osaekomi* (holding techniques), *shimewaza* (strangling techniques), *kansetsuwaza* (armlock techniques), *atemiwaza* (striking techniques), and much more.

I was an eager student. I learned by adhering to the Japanese principle of practice and repetition. After several months of intensive training and practicing and participating in tournaments, I was promoted to the rank of *sanku* (brown belt).

By now, my sensei had singled me out as one of his top pupils in judo. Not only did I trust and respect him as my sensei, but we trusted each other as friends. Now whenever he was assigned to ride with me on highway patrol during the day shift, he would tutor me in basic Japanese, especially judo terms. In addition, he taught me some of the special self-defense techniques used in the Okinawan police academy. Often, I would say to myself, I've got the best of two worlds!

After several months of training in judo and self-defense, I became more confident as an armed forces policeman. One night as my partner and I were patrolling one of the towns that GIs often frequented, we noticed one of the armed forces town patrol policemen waving for us to give them some assistance in a particular bar where several GIs were becoming disruptive.

We parked our patrol car and walked into the bar. The first thing we noticed was a marine and a sailor going after each other both verbally and physically. The marine appeared to be the most aggressive. I said to myself, *Here we go again.* Knowing that the best way to stop a fight is to try to separate the aggressor from his opponent, I approached the marine and said, "Stop fighting or we will have to take you back to your base."

He whirled around and looked at me, dressed in my blue air force uniform, my billy club on my left side, and my 45-caliber in a holster on my right side, and said, "Ain't no fly boy gonna tell me to leave town."

Immediately after his verbal defiance, I became his target: he lunged at me with a roundhouse punch. Suddenly, my judo training came into play. I, the one who had just been called a "fly boy," went into action: I ducked under his right-hand punch and executed a *kata-guruma* (shoulder wheel throw) on him. He landed behind the bar, shattering glass bottles along the way, as the owners scrambled from behind the bar with smiles of satisfaction.

Again, as was customary, we told the owners that the military would take care of the damages done to their place of business. Needless to say the defiant and subdued marine was taken back to his base and dealt with accordingly.

It was funny how quickly the news of the incident traveled throughout the military bases on Okinawa. After that, all the GIs gave me a nickname: "the little tiger." In each town where I patrolled after that, the GIs would whisper upon seeing me, "Guys, you better cool it; the little tiger is on duty tonight."

Upon hearing the news about how I had handled myself during my latest encounter with a marine, my sensei called me into his office and told me that he was pleased with my dedication and hard work in judo training. He shook my hand and said, "You're *joto* [good] in judo. I want you to attend our judo headquarters and be tested for black belt."

Approximately two weeks later, my sensei took me to the judo headquarters to be tested for promotion to black belt. I was tested in each phase of judo. Fortunately, my sensei had taught me the Japanese name of each technique. As they tested me, the judges called out the techniques in Japanese. In response I had to demonstrate each technique. I passed each phase of testing and was promoted to the rank of Shotokan (first degree black belt), issued by the Kodokan Judo Institute in Tokyo.

A few weeks later I completed my nearly eighteen-month tour of duty on Okinawa. I was told by the personnel officer in charge that I was scheduled to fly back to the United States on a Flying Tigers airline plane, rather than traveling by ship. Upon hearing this news, I was one happy airman, because I had not been looking forward to spending another nineteen days sailing on a ship.

As I was on the plane on the way back to the United States, I began reflecting on my tour of service on Okinawa. I thought about my sergeant friend who had encouraged me to sign up for armed forces police duty and how it had led me to meeting my Okinawan sensei, who taught me judo and self-defense. These two men, one American and the other Okinawan Japanese, will forever stand out in my mind as special heroes in my life: they said words to me and did things for me that encouraged me to go forward. I will forever be grateful to them, for they showed me how to find the hero within myself.

Judo became an integral part of my life. By now I realized that I had awakened the awareness of the "physical hero" in me. However, I became more and more aware that it was time for me to discover the "intellectual hero" within. I remembered what my mother had told me: "Education is one of the keys that unlocks the door to knowledge." For this reason, I had been saving money for college for nearly four years while in the service.

Now I was back in the United States. In a few months I would complete my four-year duty in the US Air Force. I was scheduled to be discharged on October 5 of that year. Someone had told me that it was possible that I could be discharged one month early to begin college that September by getting a letter of acceptance from the college of my choice. With this in mind, I spoke to the sergeant in charge of my assigned air police squadron. "Sergeant, I am planning to get discharged one month early so that I can begin going to college in September. Where do I get the paperwork for that?"

The sergeant looked me in the eyes with a defiant look of superiority and said, "Airman, you are about as close to college right now as you will ever get." After catching my breath and maintaining my composure, I did an about-face and walked away from him.

Suddenly, a powerful revengeful thought entered my mind: *I'm going to show this sergeant. After graduating from college I am going to become an officer and find this sergeant and make him salute me.* Clearly this sergeant was not one of my heroes, because he did not encourage me to go forward in life.

The very next day I went to the personnel office and asked to speak to someone who could tell me about the process of getting discharged one month early to start college in September. I was told to see the adjunct personnel officer. As I walked up to the desk where the adjunct personnel officer, a second lieutenant, was sitting, I saluted him and said, "Sir, I am scheduled to be discharged the first of October, but I would like to get out one month early so that I can start college in September. How do I go about doing that?"

The second lieutenant looked at me and smiled as he said, "Here is what you do: First, you have to get written proof that you have been accepted to a college. You then return it to me and I will help you fill out a form. You will sign it and I will sign it, and then, you will take it to your squadron sergeant and have him sign it."

I saluted the lieutenant and said, "Thank you, sir."

After obtaining my high school records, I mailed them along with my letter of application to several colleges. Two weeks later, I received a letter of acceptance to one of the colleges of my choice. I immediately took a copy of it to the adjunct personnel office. The officer looked at it with an approving smile and said, "Okay, let's fill out the form. You sign it, and then I will sign it. After that, you will take it to the squadron sergeant and have him sign it, and you will be on your way." He shook my hand and said, "I am sure you will do well. Good luck." I was so happy, I almost forgot to salute. Finally, after gaining my composure, I saluted the officer, made an about-face, and headed for the door with the treasured papers in my hand.

Shortly thereafter, I was able to locate my squadron sergeant to give him the form to sign. As he looked at it, he saw that the adjunct personnel officer had signed it already. Hesitantly, he signed it and handed it back to me. I looked him directly in the eyes after receiving the papers in my hands and said, "Thank you, sergeant." As I walked away, I said to myself, *There is more than one way to skin a cat.* Within a few days, I was honorably discharged from the US Air Force. After taking a few days off, I enrolled in college. It was the beginning of another search, this time for the intellectual hero within.

CHAPTER 4

Searching for the Intellectual Hero Within

Soon after beginning my freshman year at Wichita State University, I discovered that my high school learning had not prepared me academically. It was clear that I was lacking in the core areas of English, science, and math. However, I did have one advantage over most of the other freshmen: I was more mature and disciplined than they were, thanks to my four years in the US Air Force. The air force had taught me how to focus and maintain an attitude of "stick-to-itiveness" to find a way to get the job done.

I am thankful for the many helpful and patient teachers who assisted me in getting tutorial help and for the many helpful students who took time out to share their knowledge with me. Although I could never name them all, in my mind they were heroes who said something to me or did something for me that helped me to make it through my first year in college.

I also soon discovered that going to college was expensive. The money I had saved in the service for college was almost gone. Think about it: I didn't have a GI Bill, I didn't have a scholarship or a grant, and I didn't have a job. Nonetheless, I had determination and the will to succeed.

After enrolling for the first semester of my second year of college, it was clear that I would soon need additional funds. One day while going through the school cafeteria line for my food, I saw that several students had part-time jobs working in the cafeteria. Shortly thereafter, I asked one of the boys, "Who's in charge of hiring?" He told me that an elderly lady was in charge and that he would introduce me to her.

The next day after all the students were served and the cafeteria was cleared, he introduced me to the elderly lady, one whom we called Miss Anne. She wore a hair net over her well-kept, white-gray hair and had blue eyes that had a look of compassion. After the initial greeting, she led me into her office and invited me to sit down in a chair near her desk. Sitting behind her desk, she looked at me with her compassionate eyes and said, "I hear that you're looking for a job."

"Yes, ma'am," I said.

"What kind of work experience do you have?"

Suddenly, I remembered what someone had told me about looking for a job: "Always make sure that you relate your job experience to the job you're seeking." So I said, "I was born and raised on a farm, and I am an air force veteran." I could see the look of satisfaction on her face when she heard that information. I continued, "I served on KP duty in the military service and cleaned many tables, mopped many floors, and scrubbed many dishes and ran them through the dishwashing machine."

With a reassuring smile, she said, "I could use another dishwasher right now, but there may be other openings in the future."

"Ma'am, dishwashing is okay with me," I replied. I could see that she was pleased with my answer. She then explained how much I would be paid hourly and the hours I would be working. After that, she handed me a short form application and directed me to fill it out and sign it. She said she would process the application and contact me in a few days. Several days later she called me and told me I could start working the next day.

I reported for work the next day. After several weeks working as a dishwasher, I was promoted to cleaning up the whole cafeteria with one other student under my supervision. It was a job that allowed me to work nearly six hours a day, by scheduling most of my classes during the morning hours.

I was able to work at this job for nearly two years. It helped make it possible for me to stay in college. I will forever be grateful to this elderly lady, who became a mother figure to me. Surely this was a pivotal point in my college career. And it all happened because this elderly lady, who was the head of the school cafeteria, gave me a job when I needed it. She was a hero in my life. It is another reminder that heroes come from all walks of life.

Midway through my second year in college it became clear that I had to reevaluate my goal of getting a degree in engineering. Making passing grades became increasingly difficult. Courses in advanced math and other related engineering courses were causing my grades to begin to go south. This was in part because my high school background had not prepared me for these types of courses. I wanted to become an engineer—so much so that I could taste it. However, I saw the writing on the wall, so to speak. I realized that it would take six years or more and much money to get a degree in engineering.

After pondering what to do, I remembered what one of my high school teachers had told me: "Always have a goal in your life, but don't be afraid to change goals if necessary."

Upon looking for other options, I discovered that I could transfer to the technology education curriculum and get a degree in education. I further discovered that I had already taken enough math to get a minor in it, and in addition, I had already taken enough drafting and mechanical drawing classes to fulfill one of the electives in industrial technology. I changed my major from engineering to industrial technology with a minor in math.

During my junior year in college, the professor who taught the metalworking class in which I was a student told us that he also worked at the Boeing Company in Wichita, and that it was just one of four airplane companies in the Wichita vicinity: there was also Beechcraft, Cessna Aircraft, and Lear Siegler. He went on to tell us that as he was studying for a degree in technology education, he had worked from 3:00 p.m. to 11:00 p.m. while taking morning classes.

At the end of the class period, I approached him and explained that I would like to apply for a metalworking job at one of those companies. He told me Beechcraft was advertising for jobs in the sheet-metal department. I said to him, "I sure would like to inquire as to whether they have a three-to-eleven p.m. shift."

With an encouraging tone in his voice, he said, "Once they find out you're an air force veteran and a technology education student in your junior year, I believe you will have a good chance of getting a job at Beechcraft. I suggest you go and apply as soon as possible. And by the way, you can use me as a character reference."

Excited, I shook his hand and said, "Thank you, sir. I'm going there tomorrow."

That afternoon, I reported to the cafeteria for work as usual. I had pondered in my mind how I would mention to miss Anne, my "adopted mother," for whom I had worked almost two years, that there was a job opening at one of the airplane companies for which I wanted to apply. Finally, I decided I would approach her in a hypothetical way. I reported for work early that day, because I wanted to ask her opinion in private. After my "How are you doing today?" greeting, I said to her, "Ma'am, I need to talk to you in private. Could we talk in your office?"

She said yes and beckoned me toward the office. Once in the office, I said, "I read an advertisement in the paper that one of the airplane companies is hiring. Do you think I should apply?"

She paused for a moment and said, "I hear the airplane companies pay well. If I were you, I would go and apply."

Trying to maintain my composure, I said, "I will feel kind of sad leaving here because you've been so good to me."

With tears in her eyes, she said, "We'll be all right. You go and get that job."

We hugged each other, and as I tried to hold back my tears, I said, "I'll come back to see you as soon as I find out what happens."

Waving to me, she said, "Boy, get outta here and go make some money so that you can finish college!"

"Yes, ma'am ... Yes, ma'am, I will ... I will!" I said as I left.

The next day after finishing my morning classes, I drove to Beechcraft's personnel office. Upon arriving I introduced myself to the receptionist and asked her to direct me to the personnel officer in charge of hiring in the sheet-metal department.

The receptionist picked up the phone and said to the person on the other end, "There is someone here who would like to speak to you about the sheet-metal jobs."

Minutes later, she directed me to his office. After introducing myself, I mentioned that I was there to inquire about the sheet-metal jobs. The man asked, "Do you have any experience in sheet-metal fabrication?"

"After serving four years in the US Air Force, I enrolled in Wichita State University, home of the Wheatshockers, and I am currently in my junior year studying for a degree in technology education," I said. "I have taken several courses in metalworking that included sheet-metal layout work and fabrication. In addition, I have experience in running sheet-metal fabrication machines, as well as lathes and milling machines."

As I was talking, I noticed that my mentioning that I was a veteran of the US Air Force seemed to put a special sense of satisfaction on his face. He said, "It sounds like you might qualify." He handed me an application to fill out. After I filled out the application, he briefly examined the information I had provided and seemed satisfied. He then took me to another room and directed me to take a written exam. After I had completed the written exam, he graded it and said with a smile, "You did well on the exam. We have an opening on the three-to-eleven p.m. shift. When can you start?"

Restraining my excitement, I answered, "Sir, I can start tomorrow."

He shook my hand and said, "Congratulations: you got the job. Report here tomorrow at one thirty, and we'll take it from there."

After shaking his hand, making sure I did not use a judo grip, I said quickly, "Thank you, sir. I'll see you tomorrow." As I drove back to campus, I remembered what I had once heard an old country preacher say: "The Lord will make a way somehow!"

As I said earlier, upon entering college I did not have a GI Bill, a scholarship, or grants—just the little money I had saved while serving in the air force for four years. Working in the cafeteria when school was in session and working various jobs during the summer enabled me to somehow stay in school my freshman and sophomore years. Needless to say, landing a full-time job at Beechcraft gave me a renewed hope of finishing my undergraduate degree. Now I could see a glimmer of light at the end of the tunnel, so to speak. This new job would make it possible for me to live off campus and attend school full-time.

After one year at Beechcraft, I was promoted to the position of lathe operator in the machine shop, where I was able to work until I graduated from college with a bachelor's degree in technology education. Surely this was another milestone in my life. Without the help and encouragement of those heroes whom God placed in my path, it would not have happened.

I cannot speak for others, but for me, getting that first college degree at the undergraduate level was the most difficult. As I reflected on those early years in college, I said to myself again, I owe my success to the heroes that God placed in my life: the ones who said something to me or did something for me that encouraged me to move forward.

After receiving my degree in technology education, the same teacher who had informed me about the Beechcraft job contacted me and told me the Boeing Company was hiring college graduates. He suggested I go to their personnel office and fill out a job application, and said I could use his name as a reference. Given that he was already employed there, he said, might help. The next morning, with my degree in hand, I went to Boeing and filled out an application. The person who interviewed me looked at my application, which included my job experience at Beechcraft, my four years in the US Air Force with an honorable discharge, and a bachelor's degree in technology education. He opened a book that appeared to list several job openings. Lifting his hand to his chin, he said, "Umm ... umm. I believe I have a job for your qualifications. We have an opening in the B-47 engineering modification program for a fabrication planning engineer."

After explaining the starting rate and the benefits provided, he went on to say, "The first two weeks, you will receive training with pay, and after that you will be assigned to work under the supervision of one of the senior planning engineers. If you are interested, we will assign you on the day shift."

Without hesitating, and while trying to present an air of assurance, I said, "Yes, sir. I accept the offer."

He extended his hand, and as we shook, he instructed me, "Report here tomorrow at eight a.m. and we will get you processed in."

I replied, "Thank you, sir. I'll see you tomorrow morning."

The next morning I reported to personnel and was processed in, with the agreement that I would report for work two days later. By now, I was elated—so much so that it had not sunk in that my dream of working in engineering was still coming true; it all seemed so surreal! Can you imagine me working in engineering? Think about it: I had always wanted to be an engineer. Although

I did not have a degree in one of the common disciplines in engineering, here I was, getting ready to work in engineering!

Later on, I drove from Boeing to Beechcraft, just on the other side of town. Out of respect and appreciation I wanted to say thanks to them for employing me for nearly two years while giving them notice that I had accepted a job in engineering that was to begin in two days. They congratulated me and expressed their appreciation for giving them advanced notice. After saying good-bye, I thought about what my father once told me: "Son, don't burn your bridges behind you, for you never know when you might have to cross over them again."

Working at Boeing was an exciting and rewarding time. After working in the B-47 engineering modification planning department for a year, I was called to the personnel office and informed that the numerical control engineering department had several openings for trainees. I had heard about numerical control, but I wanted to know exactly what it entailed. Realizing I wanted more information, the personnel officer took me to the numerical control department's office and introduced me to the manager. The manager explained to me that numerical control involves writing computerized programs for numerical controlled machines in the machine shop for the purpose of manufacturing aircraft parts.

Then he said, "Come and let's take a tour through the numerical control programming area and its training department. After that, I'll take you down on the floor to observe some of the computerized machines machining some of the aircraft parts using the numerically programmed tapes." I was awed at what my eyes saw: the huge machines machining metal parts, some three-axes, and some five-axes, at maximum speed. The manager saw that I was somewhat overwhelmed; smiling, he said, "It'll take you a while to get used to this."

Upon returning to the office, he said, "We noticed in your job application and résumé that you have a strong math background, a strong mechanical drawing background, and a strong metalworking background. In addition, you have operated a metal cutting lathe in one of the other aircraft companies. Therefore, we believe you may qualify for one of the trainee jobs in numerical control programming. We'll assign you to a senior programmer during the first six hours each day, and then you'll attend a numerical control programming training school for the remaining two hours for a period of three months. Upon successfully completing the training program, you will be classified as a junior numerical control programmer. Would you like to give it a try?"

Clearly this was another opportunity for advancement. I responded to the manager by saying, "Yes, sir."

It's amazing what one can learn when one has the right attitude for learning: seeing a need for learning, desiring to learn, learning, and giving the proper feedback with an attitude of gratitude for the privilege of learning. It was not only a promotion for me but also provided me with the opportunity to be exposed to the early computers, such as the old Univac 1100 series and the IBM 360s. It was an introduction to the increasingly digitized world.

I had become so pleased with my employment at Boeing that I was saying to myself, I will always have a job here.

Well, in my naïveté, I did not know that companies such as Boeing have to depend on both commercial and government contracts. Soon afterward, reality took a front seat. I'll never forget the day. I reported to my department as usual to begin my daily programming activity. I was told to report to the personnel office along with many other workers, where we were politely told that we were being laid off with a promise of rehire if things picked up. I had never been laid off before. It was one of the worst feelings I have ever had. It is something that one cannot explain. You see, if you have never been laid off, you do not know the feeling.

But thanks be to God, I have always taken pride in my comeback power. I began looking for alternative employment. Through a contact person I discovered that Cessna Aircraft, another aircraft company in Wichita, had a job opening in the engineering scheduling department. I asked my contact person, "Do they have a numerical control department?"

He said, "Yes, but they are not hiring. I suggest you apply for the scheduling job."

"Thanks," I said. "I'm going to the personnel office tomorrow."

The next day I drove to Cessna Aircraft and applied for the scheduling job. Upon filling out a job application and providing a résumé, I was interviewed by the supervisor of the scheduling department, who told me that the scheduling job I was applying for was called PERT (Program, Evaluation, and Review Techniques), and that it involved making activity charts of all the engineering activities, showing a time line of each. The progress of each set of engineering activities had to be monitored by the schedulers.

He then took me on a tour of the scheduling department to get a firsthand look at schedulers in action. I was impressed. After further questioning me about my résumé, he said, "I see that you have some background experience in computer programming as well as in planning. I think you can fit in." After he paused for a moment, he asked me, "Do you think you can handle it?"

Making sure I maintained a look of confidence, I respectfully looked him in the eye and said, "Yes, sir, I am confident that I can handle it."

He accompanied me back to personnel and told them, "We want him to start tomorrow." He turned and shook my hand and said, "I'll see you tomorrow at eight a.m."

I nodded as I responded, "Thank you very much. I'll see you tomorrow." As I was driving back home, overflowing with joy, I said to myself, *God is still placing heroes in my path; surely His angels are watching over me.*

The scheduling job at Cessna was indeed a great learning experience. It was a job that gave me the opportunity to monitor all of the engineering activities, from the drawing board, through all the engineering activities, manufacturing, procurement, and testing, to the first "fly date" of the prototype of a small business jet.

We watched the test pilot taxi down the runway, revving up the engines of the plane as it headed forward, gaining speed. It lifted its nose gear, gradually rose into the air, and leveled off, flying through the sky. We all gave out a loud cheer, for it was a successful flight. It was a proud time for all of us.

However, it wasn't long before Cessna, like the other aircraft manufacturers, began to cut back on its workforce because its number of customer contracts declined. One of my coworkers in scheduling and I began talking one day as we went for a coffee break. He asked me, "Did you tell me that you worked at Boeing as a numerical control programmer?"

"Yes," I said.

He began to explain that he had worked as a consultant (also known as a job shopper) planning engineer for several companies. "I made big money," he said, "and I recall that the numerical control programmers with whom I worked made more than I did." Then he paused and said, "I heard that Grumman Aircraft on Long Island is hiring consultant planners and numerical control programmers. I'm going to apply. I suggest you write a good résumé. I'll give you some names of consultant companies that take care of the hiring. Send your résumé to them and see what happens."

Of course, I was excited about the prospect of making a lot of money. I sent my résumé to several consultant companies. Within a few days a representative from one of the companies called and told me he had a job for me as a numerical control programmer at Grumman Aircraft Corporation. After getting more detailed information, I told him that I needed to speak to my wife before accepting the offer. It was a big move, because I had to leave my family behind until I settled in New York.

My wife and I discussed the move: I told her I would be making a lot of money, and that once I got settled in the job,

I would move her and our daughters to New York. Well, the big money and the excitement of moving to New York made quite an impression on her. She encouraged me to try it and see whether I liked it. I called the consultant company and had the representative call and make arrangements for me to report for work at Grumman ten days later. I told the consultant company I would inform Cessna that I was leaving for another job. After giving Cessna's personnel official my notice, I immediately called the consultant company to get in touch with Grumman and confirm my expected report date.

I was told that if I drove, I would have to travel through parts of New York City to get to Long Island. I also was told that the best way was to take the George Washington Bridge into the Cross Bronx Parkway and that I could take one of three bridges onto Long Island. After an overnight stop in Ohio, I awakened early the next morning and headed for New York, arriving about 9:00 p.m. As I started across the George Washington Bridge, I could see the bright lights of New York City. As I drove across the bridge and entered the Cross Bronx Expressway, I glanced at my gas gauge and realized I needed to purchase more gas to ensure that I made it to Long Island. At the next exit I drove to the nearest service station and filled my tank with gas. After paying the attendant, I asked, "What is the best bridge to take to get to Long Island?"

The attendant answered me in an apparent West Indian accent, "The best way to get to Long Island is to take Frogs Neck Bridge."

"Thank you very much," I said as I began driving off. As I drove along the Cross Bronx Expressway, I noticed a sign that said "Triborough Bridge to Long Island." Well, I remembered what the attendant had told me: take the Frogs Neck Bridge. So I said to myself, *I'm going to continue until I see the sign that says Frogs Neck Bridge.*

I continued driving, and a few miles later I saw a sign that said "Throgs Neck Bridge to Long Island, New York." After pondering this for a few moments, I said to myself, *That fella at the service station said to me what sounded like "Frogs Neck Bridge," but I think I had better take "Throgs Neck Bridge."* Well, sure enough, I was right: Throgs Neck Bridge took me right into Queens, which led me to Interstate 495 East onto Long Island. It was a reminder to me that it also helps to be able to interpret different accents, too.

Working at Grumman Aircraft Company on Long Island as a numerical control programmer taught me that each aircraft company has its own unique way of doing things. I soon discovered that they were using the IBM 360 series computers. I was reminded of a simple definition of intelligence: "It is the ability to adapt." Well, it didn't take me long to adapt. It was a challenging job, in part because there were so many short-term deadlines to meet. Nevertheless, It was a good-paying job, especially with all the overtime. By now, I had learned to check on what type of contract the company had. As a result of my inquiring I discovered that Grumman depended primarily on government contracts. However, the navy fighter jet program I was working on had a long-range contract that was projected to last for several years.

After about six months, I moved my family to Long Island. Many of my fellow numerical control programmers who were also working as consultants often talked with me about how they had worked for aircraft companies from California to Maine. I am reminded of what one of these consultant engineers said to me: "If you are going to make a career of this type of work, you better be willing to travel a lot, because they only keep you as long as there is work available. They can let you go anytime."

CHAPTER 5

Searching for the Intellectual Within and Being a Hero for Others

Upon hearing what one of my fellow consultant programmers had said about making a career in that line of work, I thought about the fact that I had just moved my family to New York. I said to myself, *I don't think I want to make working as a consultant programming engineer a career, and in the process, move my family from place to place.* I couldn't stop thinking about it. It was as if a resounding voice from within was saying to me over and over again, "Remember, you have a degree in technology education. You have been called to be an educator. Go and teach."

The idea of teaching was growing stronger and stronger in my mind. I began thinking about the importance of teaching. Teaching is a special ministry. Teaching is one of the most important jobs in our society. When you teach, you touch lives! Teaching is about more than training or conveying information. It is about inspiring the students to move forward in life. Suddenly, the thought hit me: Think about it. You have been searching for heroes in your life. Now it's time for you to be a hero in your students' lives. Don't you remember that heroes are people who say something to others or do something to others that encourages them to go forward in life? I answered my own question: Yes!

The idea of teaching became stronger and stronger in my mind, especially when I considered that teaching jobs are some of the most stable in our society. Plus, teaching would be an ideal job to have when raising a family. I began collecting the necessary documents for applying to the New York State Education Department for certification to teach. I wrote a résumé with a letter of introduction and mailed it in, along with my college transcript and a sealed copy of my technology education degree.

Although I was very much aware that some states have different requirements for teachers in general, and that I might have to take additional courses to qualify in New York, I also knew that a technology education degree is known as a generic degree. I said to myself, *Just maybe New York State will certify me outright, without my having to take additional courses.*

Within ten days, I received a folder from the New York State Education Department. Enclosed was a certificate to teach technology as well as K–12 mathematics, in which I had a minor. With joy in my heart, and a renewed realization that God opens doors for us along the way, I was again ready to walk through another door in life. A voice within reminded me, "If we walk through them and acknowledge God along the way, He will surely direct our paths."

Shortly thereafter, I compiled a résumé, making sure that it was related to education, and wrote a cover letter of introduction to go with it. I mailed copies of them, along with sealed copies of my technology degree and copies of my New York State certifications, to several school districts on Long Island as well as in New York City. I anxiously waited for a letter of reply or a phone call from one of them. I was praying that I could get a job near my home in Bay Shore.

Within a few days I received a letter that was an answer to my prayer in many ways. It was from the Brentwood School

District acknowledging having received my letter of application and inviting me to call them to make arrangements to come in for an interview. I arranged for the interview, which was held the next day. First I was interviewed by the personnel manager of the district. Then I was interviewed by the principal and the department head at one of the schools in the Brentwood School District. I had had enough experience to tell whether or not an interview went well, and in my mind, the interviews went well. I was told they would be contacting me in a few days. I thanked them for their consideration. Upon returning home, I checked the odometer in my car to measure the distance between the school at which I would possibly be working and my home. It was about 1.8 miles. I said to myself, *This is too good to be true.*

I told my wife that the interview had gone well, and that they had told me they would be contacting me soon. No sooner had I said that than the phone rang. I answered it, and the voice on the other end said, "Congratulations: you have been selected for the technology education job. Could you come in tomorrow morning at nine and sign the necessary papers, along with the teaching contract? After you have been processed in, you will be assigned to your classroom."

After catching my breath, I said, "Thank you very much. I'll see you tomorrow at nine."

It was the beginning of nearly thirty years as an educator in the New York Public School System. It did not take me long to realize that as schoolteachers, we are entrusted with young people's lives—not just their education by conveying information, but also their safety and well-being. We, as teachers, are with our students for at least six hours a day during the school year, *in loco parentis* (in place of the parent). It is an awesome responsibility. But I was committed to the task.

During my thirty years as a teacher in the Brentwood schools, I was often asked by some of the other teachers, "Why do you want to teach in a school that's only five minutes from where you live?"

My answer: "One of the main reasons is that I want to be a part of their community. I want to 'sit where they sit,' so to speak." I realize that in today's society it is not in vogue for teachers, in most cases, to live in the same community in which they teach. However, I think I decided to do so because I remembered that most of my teachers during the time I attended school in Alabama stayed in our community. They shopped at the same stores where we shopped, and they attended the same churches we attended. They knew our parents and where we lived. When I think about it, I believe that had a lot to do with students not causing trouble in school.

And guess what? Right there in the Brentwood School District, I lived, shopped at the same stores, and went to the same church as some of my students and their parents. I was one of them, living in the community. It was a rewarding experience for me, although there were challenges along the way. But I never forgot what one hymn writer said: "If I didn't have any problems, I wouldn't know God could solve them."

Two incidents stand out in my memory. Most of the students knew that I was a Christian. However, some of them also somehow concluded that I was a preacher. Therefore, some asked me questions or made statements to solicit what they thought would be religious answers. I remember one day a student said in class, "Teacher, I don't believe in God."

I simply responded to him by asking a rhetorical question: "Who made the trees?"

A second incident along this same line happened one day when the principal called and told me that he had a parent of one of my students in his office and wanted to talk with me. After getting another teacher to cover my class, I went to the principal's office and was introduced to the child's father. The father said, "My son says you preach in class."

"No, I don't preach in class," I said. "I have a curriculum to teach."

"Do you ever use the word *God*?" he asked.

"Yes, every morning when we recite the Pledge of Allegiance to the Flag of the United States. And during the seventh-inning stretch of some major-league baseball games, I participate in the singing of 'God Bless America.'"

"Uh ... that's different," he said. "By the way, I'm an atheist."

At this juncture, I felt this man was trying to cast an aspersion on my integrity. Nonetheless, I said to him politely, "I have a problem with someone who says they do not believe in God and at the same time tries to explain who God is or what preaching is. Sir, I don't preach in class. However, I don't apologize for being a Christian. My job is to teach my curriculum. And by the way, your son does not come to class prepared to take notes. I would appreciate it if you would tell him to be more attentive and follow my directions. Your son has the potential to do well in class. And, oh yes, I invite you to check with my principal and afterward come and sit in the class your son is attending."

As our conversation ended, the father said with a smile, "I am satisfied that my son will do well in your class." After shaking our hands, he said to the principal and me, "Thanks for talking with me."

After he left the principal's office, I said to the principal, "I hope you know you set me up."

He smiled and said, "You handled it well, and I am sure his son will do well in your class from now on."

During my nearly thirty years in the New York school system, I had the privilege of teaching both mathematics and technology education classes. However, with my background in engineering and manufacturing I was able to teach students in the technology education classes in a way that allowed them to be exposed to the "head, heart, and hands" approach. It afforded them the opportunity to develop the ability to create and design, plan, and build a group project or an individual project. It was a joy to see young people, boys and girls, use their reading, writing, and mathematics skills, along with their hands-on skills, to create tangible projects. It provided an immediate reward experience for them. Although other classes such as English, mathematics, social studies, and foreign languages are very important, oftentimes students don't see the immediate rewards during their school years. That is, they often do not see the benefits of their learning until they have entered the world of work.

For this reason, technology education classes are ideal for some of our special-needs students also: they provide an opportunity for immediate reward. For example, my students would often ask if they could take their completed projects to their other classes so that other teachers and students could see them. Of course I would say yes. It gave me joy each time I saw students leave my class with their projects held up high in their hands as they walked down the hallways, heading for their next class. Sometimes I would hear other students say to them, "That's nice. Did you make that?" And the student, still holding his or her project up high so everyone could see it, with a sense of pride, would say, "Yes, I made it in my technology class!"

CHAPTER 6

Continuing the Search for the Intellectual Hero Within: Graduate Studies at New York University

It was time for me to study for a postgraduate degree. I was matriculated at New York University. From the outset, I realized that my graduate studies were going to be easier than working on my undergraduate degree. There were several obvious reasons for this: (1) as a veteran of the military, I was financially supported by the new GI Bill, (2) my school salary was another source of income, and (3) the undergraduate studies had given me a foundation.

Traveling to New York University from Long Island was a special experience in and of itself. Each day for two years, I traveled to New York University, after having met my teaching obligations from 8:00 a.m. to 3:00 p.m., to attend night classes. As I traveled back and forth by car, I was awed by the vastness and beauty of the city, with its five boroughs largely separated by bodies of water. New York City, to me, exuded a mystique like no other city. In visiting New York City on a regular basis, one could not help but notice that it included a mosaic mixture of people from all walks of life. As I traveled on the Long Island Expressway to the Brooklyn-Queens Expressway, across the Williamsburg Bridge and along Bowery Street, I often noticed the homeless people, many of whom slept on the median that separated Bowery Street's eastbound and westbound directions. Continuing to New York University, I realized that I was also near Wall Street. As I saw this contrast, I would often say to myself, Life is full of contrasts.

I shall never forget how precious five minutes could be, in that if I were five minutes late starting my drive each day, I would get caught in a traffic jam that could extend my driving time by at least an hour. Then there was another challenge that often loomed before me: many days, I could not find a parking space. As a result, I would often park in a time-limited zone because I did not want to be late for my class. Well, needless to say, my parking fines sometimes amounted to more than the cost of my books. Oftentimes, I agonized at the thought of it, but I would always encourage myself by saying, *To reach your goals, sometimes you have to travel through obstacles.*

My studies at New York University provided me with the opportunity to grow in my intellectual ability. After studying there for two and a half years, I graduated with a master's degree in education and a certificate in school administration for secondary education. I was well on my way to realizing that I had reached the self-actualization stage. Yet there was a quiet, still voice within me saying, "You are growing, but you have not fully reached the spiritual self-actualization stage." It was an echoing voice that would not leave me alone.

CHAPTER 7

Becoming Aware of the Need to Grow in the Realm of Spiritual Self-Actualization

Something deep within, from my innermost being, bearing witness to my spirit, reminded me, "God has much more for you to do." I wanted to make sure I was listening to the right voice, so I prayed to God to let me know if this was His voice telling me that He had more for me to do. "Lord, I have been in the ministry of teaching young people for almost twenty years. What more do you want me to do?"

A quiet, still voice within me said, "Yes, it is good that you have been teaching young people in the public school for many years, but now I want you to preach the gospel to the whole world."

Still, I had some more questions to ask God. Like Moses, who had excuses when God called him, I said, "But God, I am not prepared for this awesome task."

The quiet, still voice within said, "I have been preparing you throughout your life for such a time as this. And I will continue to prepare you every step of the way. Go and preach the gospel."

"Is this really God speaking to me?" I asked. The Spirit of God answered my question by impressing on my spirit John 10:4–5 KJV, where Jesus says His sheep will follow Him because they know His voice, and what the Scripture says in Romans 8:16 NIV: "The Spirit Himself testifies with our spirit that we are God's children."

It wasn't long after this that I acknowledged the call into the gospel ministry, and soon after I was ordained, I was called to become a pastor in one of the churches on Long Island. As a teacher, I had already learned that "you can't teach what you don't know, and you can't lead where you don't go." With this in mind, I knew that even as I prepared to teach and preach the gospel, it is God's Spirit who anoints us to preach, and it is His Spirit who sits down with us and helps us in studying the Scriptures. I was also reminded that God tells us in 2 Timothy 2:15 KJV, "Study to show thyself approved unto God, a workman that needeth not to be ashamed, rightly dividing the word of truth." Clearly, this is a reminder that teaching God's Word is a serious undertaking, and that we must first know the truth to teach the truth.

I wanted to study to show myself approved. I also knew that to better understand what it really meant to fully enter the spiritual self-actualization stage, I needed to grow in the knowledge of who God was and who I was. By now, I also knew that serving God was about more than giving intellectual assent to who He was; I had to be fully committed to Him and realize that He controlled every aspect of my life.

I matriculated at New York Theological Seminary in Manhattan. A voice of doubt crept into my mind when I thought of having to travel to and from New York City again. It would also mean driving through the Midtown Tunnel for four years. The voice of doubt asked, "Can you do all this, and at the same time teach school during the day?" Suddenly, the Spirit of God, who brings all things to our remembrance, refreshed my memory with what is said in Philippians 4:13 KJV, and I said, "'I can do all things through Christ who strengthens me.' Yes, I can."

After matriculating at New York Theological Seminary, I attended night classes during the months I was teaching in the public school system and day classes during the summer. Attending the seminary was both a rewarding and a challenging experience. It was challenging because I was around some people who did not believe the Bible was the inspired Word of God as cited in 2 Timothy 3:16–17 NIV, which says, "All Scripture is God-breathed and is useful for teaching, rebuking, correcting and training in righteousness, so that a man of God may be thoroughly equipped for every good work." Yet these challenges were rewarding because their skepticism moved me to diligently examine God's Word for the truth. As I allowed God's Word to speak for itself through the Holy Spirit, I was forever convinced without any doubt that God is truth, and His Word is truth.

I remember the church history classes that helped me to better understand how the Bible came to us, the Hebrew and Greek that helped me to do Bible exegesis, and the other Bible-related classes that took me deeper into God's Word. After four years of challenging but rewarding studies at New York Theological Seminary, and after four years of traveling back and forth to New York City from Long Island, I graduated with a Master of Divinity degree. I now was more prepared to proclaim God's Word in truth. I not only grew intellectually, but also was better able to understand that it is God who supplies all our needs, the full spectrum, physically and spiritually, including the need for spiritual self-actualization.

Now it was time for me to be obedient to the Lord as He sent me out to minister to the world, remembering what Christ did when He called His disciples. He called them: He said, "Come." He taught them by His word and example for three years, and as He gave His last commandment to them before He ascended into heaven, He said, "Go."

While thinking on this, I said, "Lord, thank you for calling me, thank you for preparing me. Here I am: send me."

CHAPTER 8

Reflecting On My Experience as a Schoolteacher: Did the Hero in Me Show Up?

As my public school teaching years were coming to an end, I reminded myself that it was a rewarding experience for me even though I, like other teachers, sometimes wondered whether or not I'd had an effect on my students' lives. We don't often get the positive feedback from them that we're expecting, and as a result, we sometimes think we are not making a positive difference in their lives.

Well, I discovered that sometimes you may not find out until years later. For example, I had been teaching for twenty years when one summer my wife and I, along with one of our sons and his wife, were traveling to the Bahamas on a cruise. We travelled by airline to Miami to board our cruise ship. As we were processing through US Customs, we approached one of the check-in desks behind which stood a worker, who appeared to be of Hispanic descent, in her mid-thirties. As she was checking the passports, I noticed a startled look on her face as she looked at mine. As she looked at me, she asked, "Could I ask you a question?"

"Sure."

"Did you ever teach in the Brentwood, New York, School District?"

"Yes," I said.

By now, my wife, and our son and his wife, along with many others waiting in line, had begun to wonder what was going on. Suddenly she shouted, "Oh, my God, you were my technology teacher when I was in junior high school. Hey, folks, come and see one of the greatest teachers in the world!" Everyone nearby had a look of wonderment on their faces. After realizing she was causing a delay in processing the clearance procedures for others in line, she changed the startled smile on her face to a stoic look and said, "Next in line, please."

Well, as we were vacationing in the Bahamas, I was pondering what had made this former student of mine so eager to let others know that in her mind, I was one of the greatest teachers in the world. One thought kept coming to me: Could it be that I said something to this former student, or did something for her, some twenty years ago, that prompted her on that day to treat me like some kind of hero? I tried to put the thought out of my mind and let it go. But it was a good feeling to have had this happen to me, twenty years later. So, I said to myself, *Don't let go of this precious feeling.* It played a very important part in making my cruise to the Bahamas not only one of the most enjoyable but also one of the most treasured times of my life.

Upon returning from our cruise, I was in for yet another surprise from my former student. As our ship docked in Miami, we began disembarking. It soon became very clear that hundreds of other people were disembarking also; the lines were long. As my wife, along with our son and daughter-in-law, followed me down the ramp, I noticed someone waving at me as I reached the bottom step. It was my former student! She had come to personally escort me through customs.

As we walked together, she and I had more time to talk. She told me it was easy to recognize me because I looked the same as I had twenty years earlier. That in itself was enough to lift my spirit. But what touched me the most was her telling me the reason she thought I was one of her greatest teachers. "You were a teacher who always encouraged us," she said. "You made us feel like we could achieve success, you treated each one of us as a special person, and you treated us like family."

After we completed our processing, I thanked her and hugged her as I said, "Oh, by the way, you were one of my greatest students."

As we were leaving the US Customs area, my wife said, "I've never seen a former student treat one of their former teachers like this before."

And our son said, "I can't believe what I've just seen; imagine a teacher getting recognition like this!"

I looked at them and said with a satisfied smile, "Teaching does have its rewards, although sometimes you may have to wait for them to come."

As a teacher I grew not only intellectually by furthering my formal education, but also by having to study hundreds of textbooks and related readings in preparing lessons for my classes on a daily basis. And I would be remiss if I did not acknowledge that I learned from my students as well. I will always be thankful for all those who were heroes from all walks of life, who said something to me or did something for me that encouraged me to continue going forward.

As I was nearing the final years of my teaching career, I was confident that I had reached the stage of self-actualization: I felt that I had reached my full purpose in life. I had "arrived," so to speak. Yet something deep down within was telling me that there was still more than this in life. That quiet, still voice within me kept reminding me that I needed to reach higher in the realm of spiritual self- actualization, to a place to which I was led by God, one that transcends other needs in life and at the same time permeates all the other stages of our needs.

CHAPTER 9

Searching for Heroes: My Journey as an Air Force Civil Air Patrol Chaplain

God indeed was taking me to another dimension in ministry. It all started when I accepted an invitation to speak at a local church shortly after I had retired from teaching in the public school system. After I had delivered my sermon, the service was adjourned, and one of the men in the congregation came to me and introduced himself. He shook my hand and said, "Your message was very inspiring. I noticed also that as you were introduced, it was indicated that you have recently retired from teaching, and you also recently graduated from seminary with a Master of Divinity degree."

"That's correct," I answered.

"I'm a lieutenant colonel in the US Air Force Civil Air Patrol," he said. "I also work as an air traffic controller on Long Island. And I serve as this region's wing commander in the Civil Air Patrol."

"Thank you for serving our country," I responded

With a hopeful smile he said, "I know you're thinking about taking it easy in your retirement for a while, but we sure could use you as a chaplain in the Civil Air Patrol. Would you consider joining us?"

Although I had served in the US Air Force for four years, I never knew exactly what the Civil Air Patrol did. I paused for a moment and asked, "Exactly what is the function of the Civil Air Patrol?"

"Civil Air Patrol has three core missions: aerospace education, cadet programs, and emergency services. It's a voluntary auxiliary of the US Air Force. CAP serves as a subsidiary of the air force and provides help to that branch of military through its three missions," He explained.

"Since you are a seminary graduate, you have the opportunity of being appointed as a military chaplain with the rank of captain." Then, without giving me a chance to respond, he said, "There is much more to explain. I'd like to invite you to come to our cadet squadron meeting next Thursday at five thirty p.m. so you can observe some of the things we do."

By now, it was very clear that the Civil Air Patrol needed a chaplain. Suddenly, I remembered what I had heard an instructor say in a seminary class on the topic of mission work: "Our mission is wherever there is a need." "I accept your invitation," I said. "I'll see you next Thursday."

With an even bigger smile than before, he shook my hand, and said, "It was a pleasure meeting you. I'll see you next Thursday."

After arriving back home, I began wondering about what I was getting into. Again, I began to question God. "Lord, I am retired from teaching now. I just want to serve as an assistant in a local church and take it easy for a while. Should I get involved in this Civil Air Patrol thing?"

A quiet, still voice from within spoke to me as God's Spirit witnessed to my spirit: "Remember, I called you into the ministry. The whole world is your ministry. I don't retire you; I just move you from one stage to another. And remember, in whatever stage you're in, or wherever you go, 'I will never leave you nor forsake you.'"

To this solemn reminder I said, "Not my will, but your will, Lord."

I reported to the cadet squadron meeting the following Thursday as I had promised. The lieutenant colonel was waiting for me. After introducing me to the senior officers and the cadet members during the opening ceremony, he explained that I had accepted his invitation to come and observe as a guest. After each group was separated into their respective groups—marching and drilling exercises, aerospace classes, and moral leadership classes—I was introduced to the squadron commander. He, too, reminded me they did not have a chaplain. "Therefore, our moral leadership class is being taught by a nonchaplain senior member," he said. "We need a certified chaplain who can provide the needed function of spiritual, religious, and moral leadership counseling. With your broad experience in education and religious training, you would be a welcome asset to our overall cadet program. I hope you'll consider joining us."

I replied, "I certainly will give it my consideration." He shook my hand and returned to his duties of monitoring and directing the various cadet activities.

The lieutenant colonel who had invited me escorted me as we took a close-up look at all the cadet activities going on. He explained to me that the reason this squadron was classified as a cadet squadron was that the cadet program includes boys and girls ages twelve to eighteen. As he was talking, I was touched by what I saw: young boys and girls marching to their drill leader's command just like I did when I went through basic training in the US Air Force.

What impressed me most was that although some of these young cadets were not yet well coordinated, they were serious about what they were doing and willing to learn how to take orders from their leaders. They accepted the necessary discipline to be a part of the team, just like we had been taught in the regular air force. I said to myself, Wouldn't it be nice if we could incorporate this program into our public school systems?

Next, the lieutenant colonel escorted me to the aerospace education class. There I observed the senior officers teaching the cadets about the history of aerospace, the types of airplanes used in the Civil Air Patrol, and the basics of how to fly an airplane. The instructor said something that really made an indelible impression on me: "The planes we use in Civil Air Patrol at this time are small propeller types. In addition, most of these planes are owned by our senior members, who are retired military or commercial pilots. They are not only volunteering to offer their skills and knowledge in flying, but some of them are letting us use their personally owned planes." It was clear his remarks made quite an impression on the listening cadets when one of them responded, "That's cool!"

The final activity for the night before reassembling was supposed to be the moral leadership class, the specialty for which I was being recruited. The lieutenant colonel looked at me and said, "As I said before, our moral leadership class is being taught by one of our senior members who is not a chaplain. Now you can see why you could help us in this area. By the way, the air force inspectors are scheduled to inspect our squadron in six months. Chaplaincy is one of those areas they will be inspecting and rating afterward." He paused for a moment and said, "We need you."

"It is clear you need help in this area," I said.

Without waiting for me to say whether I would be able to help, he said, "I'm going to give you all the paperwork for processing into the CAP." I accepted the papers. To him this was a "yes" answer. After dismissal, he looked at me with a relieved smile as he shook my hand and said, "I'll see you next week." Clearly by now, the only answer I could give him was "I'll do my best to be here."

And yes, I did report to the squadron meeting the next week. After several weeks of processing the necessary paperwork, obtaining an endorsement from the Southern Baptist Convention, going through a background check, and being appointed as a military chaplain, ranked as a captain in the Civil Air Patrol by the US Air Force's headquarters in Montgomery, Alabama, I suddenly realized I was wearing air force blue again.

It was a rewarding journey for the next six years, mainly because I realized that I had yet another opportunity to encourage young people to go forward in life. However, I must confess that sometimes a question would come into my mind: "Why me, Lord?" And again a quiet, still voice from within would speak to me: "Remember, the blessings I have given to you are to be shared with others."

I was not only able to develop a curriculum for our moral leadership class, but also teach lessons from it to the cadets or use it when I counseled individual cadets as well as senior members. Interestingly, I found out that sometimes the senior members needed more counseling than the young cadets. There were other activities, such as weekend bivouacs, search and rescue missions, and Memorial Day parades.

Our special time of the year was our two-week summer encampment at Fort Drum army base near the scenic Thousand Islands in New York, near the Canadian border. That was when the cadets as well as senior members got exposed to a real-life military environment, living in the military barracks with its bunk beds and eating in the same cafeteria (chow hall) as the regular US Army soldiers. It was a time of intense training, one the cadets would never forget.

One event will always stand out in my mind. As a chaplain, I was required to walk through the barracks about 9:00 p.m., after the lights were turned off and the cadets were required to be in their bunks. It was my duty to walk through the barracks and counsel or pray for the cadets who asked. Keep in mind, some of the cadets were only twelve years old and this was the first time most of them had ever been away from home for two weeks, especially in this type of setting. Well, to make a long story short, on that first Monday and Tuesday, I walked through the barracks after the lights were out and asked the cadets, "Does anyone want me to talk to them or pray for them?"

Everyone responded, "No, we're fine, chaplain, we're okay." I could tell by the tone of some of the voices that some of them were trying to tough it out.

But oh, things would soon change. As I was walking through the barracks that first Wednesday night, following my normal routine, I asked, "Does anybody want prayer?"

Several cadets called, "Chaplain, come over here and pray for me."

As I approached the first bunk bed, a young cadet on the bottom bunk said, "Chaplain, I am worried about my mother, because I have not been able to talk to her for nearly three days now. I need you to pray for me." I prayed for him.

Next, the young cadet in the top bunk said, "Chaplain, I would ask you to pray for me because I don't feel good, but I am Jewish."

Suddenly, my spirit leaped in me, reminding me of the importance of prayer for Jewish people also. "It doesn't matter if you are Jewish," I said. "Prayer is for you, too. Sure, I'll be happy to pray for you." I prayed for him.

Afterward he said, "Thank you so much. You're a good chaplain." By this time every cadet in the barracks realized that it was all right to ask for prayer. And boy, they did!

The next morning as the cadets lined up to march to the cafeteria hall for breakfast, the senior adviser noticed that one of the cadets was signaling for him to come over so that he could speak to him. He said to the senior adviser, "Sir, I feel much better today. The chaplain prayed a Protestant prayer for me!"

Later, the senior adviser got an opportunity to speak to me alone and said, "Just yesterday the Jewish cadet that you prayed for was crying and complaining, saying he didn't feel well and that someone needed to take him home." With a smile he asked, "What did you do to this boy?"

"Prayer is good for all of us, my friend. I was just doing my job … just doing my job," I replied.

Each night after our first encounter, the young Jewish cadet said as I came near his bunk bed, "Don't forget me, chaplain." This young cadet made it through the two-week encampment with flying colors. In fact, he won several awards. I said to myself, *This has been a good encampment.*

The 9/11 Terrorists' Attack on New York City: Hero after Hero Responded

My experience during the tragic attack on America by foreign terrorists on September 11, 2001, is surely one I will never forget. My wife and I were lying in bed shortly before getting up for the day and preparing breakfast when the phone rang at approximately 8:55 a.m. When we picked the phone up and said hello, one of our daughters said urgently, almost to the point of screaming, "Turn on your TV to CNN. Something bad is happening in New York City. One of the World Trade Center's buildings has been hit by an airplane!"

We turned the television on. What I saw shocked me to my bones. I could not believe what I was seeing. As I gazed at the television, I could see white smoke gushing from the top part of what appeared to be the North Tower, one of the WTC buildings. I said to my wife, "I can't believe what I see." Right before my eyes, as the scene kept unfolding on television, I reminded myself, *This is only fifty miles or so from our home in Farmingville on Long Island.*

As I sat there, still watching in disbelief, at 9:03 a.m., with my own eyes I saw another plane heading into the south face of the South Tower of the World Trade Center. I said to my wife, "I see another plane heading straight for the South Tower." And then, "Boom—it has hit the South Tower!" Almost instantly, smoke began to gush from the South Tower. By now my wife and I could not take our eyes off the TV screen.

At approximately 9:22 a.m. it was reported that all bridges and tunnels into Manhattan had been closed. As I continued watching television, I looked at the clock, which showed 9:58 a.m. As I kept watching television, the South Tower of the World Trade Center collapsed right before my eyes. Moments after it collapsed, I saw tremendous gray-white clouds of pulverized concrete and gypsum rush through the streets nearby.

Suddenly the phone rang again. It was the New York City wing chaplain directing me to get in touch with the group commander and get access to the Long Island CAP group building and wait at the phone for further instruction. After contacting the group commander to open the building as directed by the New York City CAP wing commander, he told me the building would be opened for my use within a half hour. I quickly put on my uniform and grabbed a few energy bars and a small container of orange juice, along with my chaplain kit, which included a Bible. As I was leaving, it dawned on me to bring my portable television. Minutes later, I headed for the CAP group building, which was close to eight miles from my home.

Upon arrival, I quickly entered the building, plugged my portable television into a power outlet, and turned it on. I contacted the wing commander and told her I was at the CAP group building in Bohemia, on Long Island. The wing commander directed me to "sit tight" until she checked to see whether or not I needed to be deployed to another location on Long Island. "I'll call you back as soon as I get that information," she said.

"Yes, ma'am, I'll wait by the phone," I responded.

As I sat there praying within and watching and listening to the events unfolding on television, questions began coming to my mind: How could this have happened on American shores with all of its protection, in the air, on the ground, and in surrounding waters? Who would dare attack America?

By now, it was approximately 10:30 a.m. More news was coming in over the television, as reported by CNN: Another apparently hijacked plane, Flight 77, had crashed into the Pentagon building at 9:37 a.m. The South Tower of the World Trade Center had collapsed at 9:59 a.m. United Airlines Flight 93 had crashed in Somerset County, Pennsylvania, at 10:03 a.m. after hijackers and passengers fought in the cockpit.

The North Tower of the World Trade Center collapsed at approximately 10:28 a.m., and 7 World Trade Center nearby was burning as a result. Clearly, by now it seemed as if the very foundation of America was being shaken. Yes, as a chaplain, I too was sitting there shaken, but I was still holding to an unshakeable faith in God. I felt helpless. I wanted to do something to help. I remembered what I had heard an old preacher say one day: "When the world is shaking and it seems like you can't do anything about it, pray … pray … Keep on praying." I did. "Lord, I don't know why all this is happening, but you do, so I am standing on your promise in Romans 8:28 KJV, "All things work together for good to them that love God, to them who are called according to His purpose.'"

It was now approximately 11:30 a.m. The phone rang again. It was the wing commander calling back to say things were quiet on Long Island. However, she had contacted St. Vincent Hospital, on West Fifteenth Street near Ninth Avenue in Manhattan, near the World Trade Center. She said they needed chaplains to come assist their chaplains. She and I concurred that the only possible way for me to get to New York City was by train. She then asked me with a tone of solemnity, "Would you be willing to go there tomorrow to assist in counseling? They expect a lot of activity."

I paused for a moment and said, "It is my job as a chaplain to go where I am needed. Yes, I will go."

She then said she would call and tell them I would be there about 11:00 a.m. After telling me to make sure I took my Civil Air Patrol identification as a chaplain, as well as my driver's license, she finally said, "May God bless you and watch over you—and by the way, take note of all that you experience, for I am sure you will have quite a report for us afterward."

"Thank you. I will keep you posted. See you soon," I said.

At about 8:00 a.m., September 12, 2001, I boarded the Long Island Railroad train and headed for Jamaica Station. As I was meditating on what to say to those who came to the hospital for treatment, those who came looking for their family members, loved ones, or friends, or those who simply had questions about why this was happening, I thought about when the prophet Habakkuk in the book of Habakkuk prayerfully took his questions to God. He wanted to know how God could stand by and do nothing about evil. Habakkuk needed an answer. God answered by reminding him that He had an appointed time for all evil to end. Habakkuk believed in God and that He is faithful in keeping His promises.

I then thought about the book of Job where Job wanted to know why God sometimes chooses to allow good people to suffer or doesn't judge and punish the wicked in this life for the evil they commit. God reminded Job that His time is not our time. As Peter tells us in 2 Peter 3:8 NIV, "One day is with the Lord as a thousand years, and a thousand years as one day." Although Job could not always understand the ways of the Lord, or the timing of the Lord, what he had faith in was his belief that one day God will punish the wicked and reward the righteous.

Upon arriving at Jamaica Station, I boarded a train for Penn Station in Manhattan. On my way to Penn Station, it was apparent that most of the other passengers were police officers, firefighters, doctors, nurses, and emergency rescue workers—people from all walks of life from the city, Long Island, and surrounding areas. Even those who may have been looking for someone in their family, a coworker, or a friend who was in one of the World Trade

79

Center buildings were heading for Manhattan to render their service. They all had a sense of purpose, a look of determination on their faces. I said to myself, This is what real heroes do.

After arriving at Penn Station, I boarded a subway train that would take me near St. Vincent Hospital. I spoke to someone who was also traveling on the subway and told him I was trying to get to St. Vincent's to serve as a chaplain. "What street should I get off the subway?" I asked.

"I heard that lower Manhattan has been classified as a restricted area," he said. "Therefore, you will probably be required to provide proper identification to enter. I suggest you get off the subway somewhere near West Fourteenth Street and Seventh Avenue."

"Thank you for the info," I said.

As he suggested, I got off near West Fourteenth and Seventh and began walking toward West Fifteenth and Ninth. Almost immediately I was stopped by a New York City policeman. I explained to him that I had traveled all the way from Long Island and was trying to locate St. Vincent Hospital to serve as a chaplain. As I expected he said, "I'll need to see your identification." I showed him my Civil Air Patrol identification as a chaplain, along with my driver's license. After checking my identification, he handed them back to me and said, "Okay. You may proceed, sir. You're only a few blocks from the hospital; it's in that direction." He pointed.

I thanked him and continued walking. I began smelling the smoke residue still floating in the air. The smell of gypsum dust, asbestos dust, and other residue was eerily prevalent. Within minutes there was a burning sensation in my eyes, and my nose had a stinging-itchy feeling. I comforted myself by thinking, *I am sure the hospital staff will provide me with the necessary protective gear upon my arrival.*

Upon arriving at St. Vincent's, I introduced myself to the security guard and told him, "I'm a military chaplain, and I was directed to come here to assist your chaplains." After checking my identification and signing me in, he issued me a visitor's badge, picked up his phone, and asked one of the staff members to escort me to the hospital chaplain's office.

As we were talking along the way, the nurse who was escorting me said, "Only about a dozen people have come in from the World Trade Center site, and only for minor injuries." She paused, took a deep breath, looked at me, and said, "Knowing that hundreds ... thousands of people were still in those buildings, and only a dozen or so have come here for treatment, it's an eerie feeling."

I nodded in agreement and responded by saying, "Yes, indeed, it is an eerie feeling." After regaining her composure, she took me to the hospital chaplain's office.

I introduced myself to the chaplain and told him I was an Air Force Civil Air Patrol chaplain there to help. He shook my hand and said, "Oh, yes. Your wing chaplain called and informed us that you would be coming; we are happy to have you come and assist us. As strange as it may sound, it's been very quiet here so far today. But St. Vincent's has a family center nearby, and it is bustling with activity. Would you be willing to go there and serve as a counselor?"

"Sir, I am here to help in whatever way I can," I said. "Yes, it will be an honor to do so."

With a calming smile, he said, "I'll take you to security and get a special badge as a visiting chaplain representing our hospital, afterward I'll take you to the center and show you around. After that, you, along with other chaplains and clergy, will counsel anyone who requests it." Arriving at the family center, we saw that people had come from all around: New York City, New Jersey, Long Island, and Connecticut, as well as other states. He walked through the crowd with me and offered counseling to those who requested it.

After making a few rounds with me as we counseled together, he left me to counsel alone as necessary. He gave me one of his business cards and said, "If you have any questions or need to talk to me, do not hesitate to call me. I'm going to return to the hospital to make myself available there. "May God bless you with words of comfort and wisdom." He shook my hand.

"May God bless you," I said. "I'll call you if I have any questions."

Suddenly, I realized that people by the hundreds had come seeking answers. Some carried handwritten signs; some carried posters and banners with names or pictures on them. They were searching for their missing family members, relatives, friends, neighbors, and coworkers: "Missing this person." "Where is this person?" "Have you seen this person?" "Please help me find this person!" "I am looking for this person." The signs had different messages, but the purpose was the same: trying to find someone they knew who worked in the World Trade Center and vicinity. The South Tower and the North Tower, as well as the 7 World Trade Center building, forty-seven stories high, had collapsed the day before. It had not yet been determined how many people were able to escape the South Tower or the North Tower. However, there was one consolation: 7 World Trade Center's building had not been hit directly by a plane. The people in it had had time to evacuate before it collapsed, and there were no reported injuries or deaths.

Still, I was aware that hundreds of people had either lost their lives, were missing, or simply were not accounted for. With this in mind I said to myself, In counseling those who ask, what do I tell them? A quiet, still voice within me said, "Remember the training you had in your studies at the chaplaincy school at the naval station in Newport, Rhode Island." It was in this school where I was taught to let the person you are counseling do most of the talking and to always ask the person, "Would you like me to pray for you?"

As I walked through the crowd, which kept growing by the minute, I counseled scores of people during the span of about three hours. Most were receptive to my counseling and appreciative of my words of comfort and prayer. However, a few were not very receptive to counseling, but instead had questions about the necessity of prayer or where God was in all this.

An encounter with one particular person stands out in my mind. As I approached her, I noticed she was crying, with streams of tears flowing from her eyes. She was carrying a sign with a picture and words that said, "My brother is missing. Have you seen him?" After introducing myself, I asked her, "Is there anything I can do to help?"

"Yes," she said. "Can you help me find my brother?"

"Would you like me to pray with you and ask God to help you find him?" I asked.

"Pray for what?" she shouted. "If God is so powerful, why did He let this happen?"

"My dear, I wish I could answer your question, but I don't have an answer. However, what I can tell you is that God loves you, and He wants you to keep on hoping and trusting." As I walked away to continue seeking others to counsel, I thought about what we were taught about witnessing: "If you try to witness to someone and they reject you, go on to the next one."

What I witnessed that day was another reminder of how Americans will come together and support one another in times of tragedy. On that day, I saw people who, even though they needed help and encouragement, were helping and encouraging others. People from all walks of life were pitching in and helping in their own way.

Local restaurants and grocery stores were donating hot food, fruit, cookies, potato chips, sodas, and bottled water to the family center at St. Vincent's where I was counseling. I even saw some sidewalk vendors who sold items such as pretzels, bagels, sandwiches, and hot dogs give these items to people in and around the center at no charge. Although people stayed there for hours, everyone had plenty of food and refreshments. Trying to take all this in, I said to myself, Wouldn't it be wonderful if people had compassion like this for one another even in normal times?

By now, it was almost 3:30 p.m. Someone said they had heard that Penn Station might be closed by 5:00 p.m., if not sooner. Suddenly, it dawned on me that Penn Station was my only hope of having transportation back to Long Island. I did not want to be stranded in New York City. After calling St. Vincent's chaplain and thanking him for giving me the opportunity to be a part of their counseling team, I informed him that I was heading back to Long Island.

As I began walking toward the nearest subway station, I saw a city bus with a sign on it that read "Penn Station" stopping at a bus stop nearby. I ran over and stuck my head in the door and asked the bus driver, "Is this bus going to Penn Station?"

He replied, "Yes. If you're going there, come aboard."

Without hesitating, I went aboard. "How much will it cost?" I asked.

He looked at me with a smile and said, "On a day like today, we are not charging. Put your money back in your pocket and have a seat."

"Yes, sir, thank you very much," I replied. After sitting down I said to myself, This is amazing. Normally there are no free rides in New York. While trying to take all this in, I remembered what happened on the day of Pentecost, how believers shared with one another as we are told in Acts 2:44–45 NIV: "All the believers were together and had everything in common. Selling their possessions and goods, they gave to anyone as he had need."

After arriving at Penn Station, I hurried to the counter and purchased a ticket to take the train back to Long Island. As I was sitting there waiting, a message came over the Penn Station speaker system: "Attention, please; attention, please. The Empire State Building has been closed until further notice." I said to myself, Wow. Things in the city are beginning to close down. I hope I can get out of Penn Station before it closes. Suddenly, another message came over the speaker: "Attention, please; attention, please. The Long Island train heading for Jamaica Station is ready for boarding at the assigned gate. Please board immediately."

With a sigh of relief I said, "Thank God." About fifteen minutes after the train left Penn Station, another message came over the speaker system: "Attention, please; attention, please: Penn Station has been closed until further notice." Upon hearing this I said to myself, What a miracle. I got out of New York City just in the nick of time!

Soon I was on another Long Island Railroad train, leaving Jamaica Station. As I sat in my seat, I noticed several firefighters, emergency workers, and many other people who had been in the city with me all day, all of us giving of ourselves. Many of them wore clothing that had been soiled with sweat, grit, and grime from being exposed to the gypsum and asbestos dust, among other things. The firemen, especially, stood out, because their faces were also smeared with soot. And most of them, like me, hadn't used a dust mask during our serving in the city. Before arriving home, I began reflecting on what I had experienced, and what I had seen and heard. I concluded, This is what being a hero is all about: helping others in time of need. Heroes from every walk of life were moved with compassion to come together for the common good of all, forgetting about self. What a testimony this is sending to the rest of the world! I believe when others see this, they will say, in the words of Tertullian, "See how they love one another!"

CHAPTER 10

Searching for Heroes: A Lifelong Process

After the 9/11 terrorists attack, I now realized I had remained on Long Island after retiring from teaching for about seven years. In my heart I had always wanted to return home after my retirement. I often thought about an old saying: "You can take the boy out of the country, but you can't take the country out of the boy." My wife and I prayed about it, and we felt it was God's will for us to move to Alabama. Shortly thereafter, my wife and I moved to Butler, Alabama, where I was born and raised. It had been nearly forty-eight years since I had left Alabama and joined the US Air Force.

It's amazing how God can bring us full circle in life. Well, here I was back in Alabama. I immediately reflected on what my father said just before I left home to join the air force: "I want you stay here and become a businessman." I remembered my mother begging me to plow her special garden so she could raise vegetables for us to eat. I said to myself, Daddy, if I could speak to you now, I would tell you I have come back home to be a businessman in managing the land that you and Mother left us to enjoy. And yes, Mother, if I could speak to you today, I would tell you I am sorry for not always plowing the garden when you told me to, but I am back home now, and I am going raise the biggest and best garden ever just for you!

True to my word, it didn't take me long to begin "gardening" and becoming a "businessman," managing and enjoying the land that my father and mother had left us. It was on this land where my brothers, sisters and I were born and raised.

I was more ready than ever to enjoy Alabama, with its fertile soil, its long crop-growing season, its soft southern air, and its millions of stars that can be seen in its clear skies at night. How happy I was to be back home. It was a breath of fresh air!

Of course, it didn't take me long to realize that God wanted me to do more than enjoy the fruit of the land. I prayed, "Lord, you have brought me back to where my life on this earth began. Surely there must be a reason."

A quiet, still voice in me said, "God is not through with you yet." But my answer to that quiet, still voice was in the form of a question: "How will I know?" Immediately Proverbs 3:5–6 KJV came to my memory: "Trust in the Lord with all thine heart; and lean not unto thine own understanding. In all thy ways acknowledge Him, and He shall direct thy paths."

It didn't take long for me to realize that just as God had told me before, our mission field is where there is a need. Yes, there was a need to take care of everyday business and a need to tend the garden on a regular basis. But I soon realized that people who lived around me had needs, in both the natural and the spiritual sense. While helping people around me with their physiological needs, I came to realize more and more that their greatest needs were in the spiritual realm. God had blessed me abundantly throughout my life, over and over, from filling my basic physiological needs to filling my needs for spiritual self-actualization. And when God blesses us, He wants us to be a blessing to someone else. In this sense, God can use us to be heroes in other people's lives, help them in every stage of their needs, and encourage them to go forward in life.

God had fine-tuned my ability to discern the genuine needs of others. With this in mind, since returning to Alabama, I have discovered by meeting people in all walks of life, in church, and through everyday contact that God is showing me where the needs are. Furthermore, He has given me the ability to prioritize how I respond to people's needs.

I saw a need to tutor young people in mathematics, I accepted the challenge, and as a result, I began tutoring on a regular basis. At the same time, I've been making them aware of their spiritual need. I have a standard question that I ask each one of my students. "There are two things that you should do before you go to bed at night: say your multiplication tables and the Lord's Prayer. Which one of those should you stop saying when you get older: your multiplication tables or the Lord's Prayer?" They pause for a moment, realizing that I am not only their math tutor but also a pastor, and then answer by saying, "When I get older, I am going to stop saying my multiplication tables, but not the Lord's Prayer." When I hear that, a quiet, still voice inside me tells me, "Your teaching and preaching are not in vain."

CHAPTER 11

The Importance of Growing in the Spiritual Self-Actualization Realm

Leaning on my will, I had determined in my mind that I was simply going to assist other pastors in various churches rather than becoming a pastor. However, I soon found out that God had other plans for me. He showed me there was a need to become a pastor in one of the local churches. I remembered what God had reminded me over and over again, that wherever there is a need, there is a mission. I prayed, "Lord, I hear you. Not my will, but your will be done."

Soon afterward, I began pastoring in one of the local churches, which afforded me the opportunity to visit other churches. I had already seen this pattern in New York and other places I had traveled as a pastor, but now that I am in Alabama, it is becoming clearer and clearer to me that one of the real problems we have in our society, and yes, even in some of our churches, is that some people are of the mind-set that simply joining a church, putting their names on the roll, and attending church on Sunday is what it means to be a Christian. And as a result, many are going to church simply to have church, rather than realizing that true Christians are called to be the church.

Why is this the prevailing attitude of so many people? I believe it is primarily because many do not fully know who Jesus is and thereby have not reached the stage of spiritual self-actualization. Think about it: until one knows who Jesus is, they cannot fully know who they are, and they cannot know the true meaning of church—that is, they cannot know it is the body of Christ. The local church is a place where we go to worship God and to be equipped, and afterward we are to go out and serve, realizing it is on the outside of the church, in the highways and byways, where we become real heroes for God and to others.

It brings back to my memory a defining time in my life when I began to realize that I needed to see Jesus not only in the sense of a Savior but also as a Creator. Before coming to a fuller understanding of this life-changing truth, I had to understand that God is revealed to us in essentially three ways: one, God is revealed to us in His written Word, the Bible; two, God is revealed to us through His self-revelation, Jesus Christ; and three, God is revealed to us in nature. (I expand on these three revelations in chapter 12.)

Most Christians can readily see Jesus as the Savior; however, they cannot see Him as the Creator. It is my belief that until we understand that Jesus is the Creator, we cannot fully understand why He is qualified to be our Savior. How can we understand Jesus as the Creator? The answer lies in the Bible and creation itself. Journey with me as we look at what the Bible says, and what creation shows us, about Jesus, our Creator, God.

CHAPTER 12

Seeing Jesus as God the Creator and Our Greatest Hero

My Reflection on Who Created the Universe

As I reflect on my life as a little boy growing up in Butler, Alabama, near the Tombigbee River, where the Choctaw and Chickasaw Indians once roamed, I recall those special nights in November and December, when most of the leaves from the big oak and other deciduous trees had shed most of their leaves. It was then, at night, that I often gazed up at what seemed like millions of stars glittering and dancing and bobbling way up in the clear skies over Alabama.

I remembered that at the right time of the month, the full moon could be seen in the night sky, seemingly just above the treetops, along the dirt road where I lived. As children, we used to play a game called Chasing the Moon. We were naïve enough to think that we could outrun the moon. We would run toward the moon, trying to catch up with it. It seemed like the faster we ran, the faster the moon ran. Obviously, it was a losing game, but it was fun!

It was the stars in the sky that intrigued me the most. I often thought about who made the stars, moon, and sun. I would sometimes ask my father and mother, "Who made the stars?"

Their standard answer was always, "God did."

My response to their answer was always, "Yeah, but how did God make them and put them way up there in the sky? He must have had a tall ladder."

My father usually had a follow-up answer to all my questions about God's creation of living beings and things around us: "We can't answer all these questions, but God knows all things." Even then, something within me kept saying over and over, It has to be someone bigger than man.

Here I am now, many years later, after having come back home. I still gaze up into the skies at night, and I am more awed than ever before at the many stars way up in the sky. But now I know who created them, who put them in the sky, and who sustains them: God. It is mind-boggling when we think about the immensity of God's creation. It is equally mind-boggling when we think about how God reveals Himself to us.

Three Ways in Which God Is Revealed

1. **God is revealed to us in His Word, the Holy Scripture**. The inspired Word of God reveals to us who God is. Hence, we cannot begin to know who God is until we hear the Word through teaching, preaching, and studying the Bible.

2. **God is revealed to us through His self-revelation**. God's self-revelation climaxes in the appearance of Jesus, the God-man. Words revealed much about God, but the living, breathing God-man reveals even more. In Colossians 1:15 NIV, we read, "He is the image of the invisible God." Think about it: how can you have any image of something that is

invisible? Remember, the Scripture is not talking about a physical resemblance but a spiritual one.

Have you ever considered all the different pictures, paintings, and movies by man attempting to depict what Jesus looked like? If they did look like Him, we would all be tricked into vainly trying to limit who Jesus is. In Colossians 1:19 NIV, we read, "God was pleased to have all His fullness dwell in Him [Jesus]." *Fullness* means Jesus Christ is equivalent to all that God is. To see what God is like, one must look at Jesus through all of God's attributes.

I was told a story about a young boy who went to church with his grandmother. During the service, he noticed that there was a gray-headed old man standing behind the pulpit. He noticed that the preacher was so old, he could barely talk loud enough to be heard and that he appeared to be holding on to the pulpit to stand. When the service was over, the young boy, with a puzzled look on his face, asked his grandmother, "That man who was standing behind the pulpit—is he God?"

The grandmother smiled and said calmly, "No, he is not God. The God we serve never grows old."

3. **God also is revealed to us in nature.** We are told in the Scriptures, "The heavens declare the Glory of God." Romans 1:20 NLT talks about God revealing Himself in nature: "From the time the world was created people have seen the earth and sky and all that God has made. They can clearly see His invisible qualities—His eternal power and divine nature. So they have no excuse whatsoever for not knowing God."

Moreover, I believe that to understand why Jesus Christ is our Savior, we must also understand why He is our Creator. **John 1:3** tells us that Jesus, the Word, was the Creator before He became our Savior. Therefore, the understanding of Jesus Christ as our Creator is foundational to our Christian faith. Every other aspect of theology rests upon our understanding of Jesus (who is God) as the origin of life.

Jesus and the Triune God

Although the mystery of the triune God is difficult to understand, it is one of the doctrines revealed in Scripture. The word *Trinity* is not found in the Scripture, but its essence is manifested throughout it, from Genesis to Revelation. Remember, Christianity stands alone in saying that God is one essence in three persons. For example, some religions in this world say that there is one and only one God, and others say there are multiple gods. We must not be misled by what others say God is. Too often, we approach the Bible with a self-interpreting agenda: reading it and saying what we think it is or what others say they think it is. Remember, the right question in interpreting the Scriptures is What do the words of the Bible mean? rather than, What do the words mean to me? We must look for the objective meaning rather than the subjective meaning.

Remember, too, that trying to explain God within our finite understanding is like trying to explain that three equals one and one equals three. Who can fully explain God? No one. Finite man cannot fully explain the infinite God. Therefore, we must let God's Word speak for itself!

Genesis 1:1 NIV says, "In the beginning God created the heavens and earth." The Hebrew word for God is *Elohim*. *Elohim* is a plural word. It is the word used to name God throughout the entire creation chapters. Genesis 1 and 2 indicates that Christ actually created all things for the Father. All three persons of the Trinity—God the Father, God the Son, God the Holy Spirit— are evidenced in the creation chapters in Genesis and elsewhere in Scripture. All three are active in creation. The plural pronouns *us* and *our* in Genesis 1:26 are also expressing the tri-unity of

God. They are in perfect agreement at every moment. All three equal only one God in nature as cited in Deuteronomy 6:4. Jesus is the same as God in nature. The Holy Spirit is the same as God in nature. Christ has all the attributes of God the Father. He is God. He is the creator of the Universe and everything therein.

The Heavens Declare the Glory of Jesus, the Greatest Hero

When we look at the visible things created by God, we are looking at Him through the revelation of Nature. Psalm 19:1 NIV says, "The heavens declare the glory of God; the skies proclaim the work of his hands." Remember, the Bible talks about three heavens. The first two heavens are natural, and the third heaven is spiritual, where God abides. In 2 Corinthians 12:2–4, Paul identifies the place where he was taken up to paradise as the third heaven. In 1 Kings 14:11 NASB we read, "He who dies in the field the birds of the heavens will eat." This refers to the "first heaven," the sky where the birds fly. Deuteronomy 4:19 KJV says, "And lest thou lift up thine eyes unto heaven, and when thou seest the sun, and the moon, and the stars, even all the host of heaven," referring to the outer space of infinite extent, the sun, stars, moon, and other celestial objects. They all were created by God and belong to Him as cited in Deuteronomy 10:14 KJV, which says, "Behold, the heaven and the heaven of heavens is the Lord's thy God."

The "heavens declare the glory of God." The word *glory* as used in Psalm 19:1 in Hebrew means *kabowd;* it implies honor, abundance, splendor, and dignity. To speak of God's glory is to speak of His intrinsic perfection. Think about it: we can do nothing to add to or take away from God's perfection. We bring glory to God, the Creator, just by being aware of His presence.

One could write volume upon volumes of books and never fully describe the magnitude of God's creation. However, it is my belief that when we consider the stars, the moon, the sun, and the many galaxies, we can see a demonstration of a God who is eternal, infinite, omnipotent, omniscient, and omnipresent.

Even scientists, although some of them do not yet acknowledge that God created the universe, marvel at the magnitude of His creation by simply observing what they have discovered in the skies above and beyond. Astronomers have discovered that millions of galaxy clusters fill the universe, each containing thousands of galaxies. It has been estimated that within these galaxies are ten billion trillion stars, and counting. Think about it: that's ten with twenty-one zeroes after it. That in itself is mind-boggling!

The sun is the largest and most massive star in the solar system. It has a diameter of 865,000 miles, whereas the earth's diameter is only 7,918 miles. Simply put, the sun is 1,287,000 times bigger than the earth. Yet it is just a medium-sized star among the hundreds of billions of stars in the Milky Way galaxy alone. The sun is approximately 93 million miles from the earth. If the sun was too close to the earth, it would be too hot for humans and other life to live; if it was too far from the earth, it would be too cold for humans and other life to live.

No matter how vast and innumerable all the galaxies and stars, both discovered and undiscovered by scientists, each one is necessary to sustain life support here on earth. Not only that, most scientists realize that if the number of stars in both the observable and unobservable universe were any greater or any fewer, life would be impossible here on earth.

Jesus Not Only Created All the Stars in the Universe, but Also Numbered and Named Them All

Whenever I'm asked, "How many stars are there in the universe?" I humbly answer, "Only God knows." God asked Abraham this rhetorical question in Genesis 15:5 NIV, which says, "He took him outside and said, 'Look up at the sky and count the stars—if indeed you can count them.'" In Isaiah 40:26 NIV, God asked the same rhetorical question: "Lift up your eyes and look to the heavens: Who created all these?" And then He answered his own question: "He who brings out the starry host one by one and calls them by name. Because of His great power and strength, not one of them is missing." It is clear man does not know, but God knows! The Scripture tells us in Psalm 147:4 NIV, "He determines the number of stars and calls them each by name." That in itself is amazing and beyond what mere man can imagine! Think about it: He not only names and numbers the stars, but also has a unique purpose for each one.

Jesus Created the Whole Universe and Everything Therein

In Genesis 1:1 NIV we read, "In the beginning God created the heavens and earth." The phrase *heavens and earth* means all physical reality. The word *created* in Hebrew is *bara*. It implies something brand new that never existed before. Hebrews 11:3 NIV attests to this truth: "By faith we understand that the universe was formed at God's command, so that what is seen was not made out of what is visible."

Science essentially expresses the universe in five terms: *time, space, matter, power,* and *motion*. The five terms are perfectly revealed in Genesis 1:1–2 NIV: "In the beginning *[time]* God created *[power]* the heavens *[space]* and the earth *[matter]* and the Spirit of God moved *[motion]* upon the face of the waters." From the very beginning, God reminds man that He controls all aspects of the universe.

The creation chapters, Genesis 1 and 2, show God creating the whole universe in a purposeful order:

Day One

1. He created a formless planet earth suspended in the darkness and void of space.
2. He created light.
3. He created the separation of light from the darkness.

Day Two

4. He created the formation of the earth's atmosphere, separating the water into two parts: oceanic and subterranean water, and atmospheric water.

Day Three

5. He created dry land and oceans.
6. He created a system to water the entire land surface using subterranean waters.
7. He created vegetation, seed-bearing plants, and trees that bear fruit.

Day Four

8. He created the sun.
9. He created the moon.
10. He created the stars and other planets.

Day Five

11. He created water creatures of all kinds.
12. He created birds and all fowls of the air.

Day Six

13. He created land animals: creatures that move close to the ground, large animals, and animals to be used by man as livestock.
14. God made man, Adam, after His own image.
15. God formed Eve, the first woman, from Adam in His own image.

The order of God's creation was done in perfect sequence, one that was preparing it for human beings. God created the whole universe and everything therein. He made us in His image, and He has commanded us to be good stewards, that is, managers of it all. In Genesis and elsewhere in the Bible we are told to be faithful stewards in all that we are and in all that we have. Think about it: when we acknowledge that God created the whole universe and everything therein, and owns and sustains it, surely He deserves all the praise and all glory belongs to Him alone. What a mighty God we serve!

Jesus is our Creator. Isaiah 45:5–22 stipulates that God alone is designer and creator of the whole universe.

In John 1:1–3 KJV, we read, "In the beginning was the Word, and the Word was with God, and the Word was God. He was with God in the beginning. Through Him all things were made; without Him nothing was made that has been made."

Colossians 1:16 NIV reminds us, "For by Him [Jesus] all things were created: things in the heaven and on earth, visible and invisible, whether thrones or powers or rulers or authorities;

all things were created by Him and for Him." Yes, Jesus is God. He is the Creator of the universe!

How Did Jesus Create the Whole Universe?

From the outset, it is important to understand that the human mind with its limited knowledge cannot fully understand how God created the universe. However, we have the assurance that God's Word is truth as cited in 2 Timothy 2:15.NIV. It is faith in God and His Word that helps us understand the things of God. Hebrews 11:3 NIV says, "Through faith we understand that the universe was formed at God's command, so that what is seen was not made out of what is visible."

Why is faith so important? The answer is given in Hebrews 11:6 NIV, which says, "And without faith it is impossible to please God, because anyone who comes to Him must believe that He exists, and that He rewards those who earnestly seek after Him." So the starting point is believing that God exists. And if we earnestly seek Him in faith, we have the assurance that He is faithful and can do all things, including rewarding us for our faith. It is a faith that gives us the ability to spiritually discern who God is and what He can do.

The creation chapters, Genesis 1 and 2, say, "And God said." God spoke the universe into existence as also cited in Psalm 33:6 NIV, which says, "By the word of the Lord were the heavens made, their starry host by the breath of His mouth." Notice that the Scripture tells us in Ezekiel 12:25 NIV what God says: "But I the Lord God will speak what I will, and it shall be fulfilled without delay ... declares the Sovereign Lord."

Think about it: in Genesis we read that God spoke the universe into existence, and in Revelation we are told that Jesus will speak the word and Satan and all his followers will be defeated. He will speak the word and the whole universe will be judged and purged. Second Peter 3:10–13 reminds us that the present order of things will be annihilated by God's judgment and replaced by a new heaven and a new earth. God had the first say and He will have the last say. God cannot lie: if He says it, He will do it. The book of Revelation speaks to this truth.

Jesus Is in Control of the Expansion of the Universe

With the invention of the Hubble Telescope and other advanced technologies, more and more scientists are beginning to discover that the universe is expanding, or stretching out. Although science can attempt to explain "how" the universe is expanding, only God can explain the "why." He is expanding the universe to maintain life for His creatures here on earth, and it's because He loves us and cares for us.

Let us look at Psalm 147:4 NIV again: "He determines the number of the stars and calls them each by name." The word *determines* as used in Psalm 147:4 is in the present tense. It is safe to say that God is continuously determining and naming the stars, as well as controlling their distance from each other. Energy and gravity, which God created—all of these factors come into play with the rate of expansion and so forth.

I am reminded what a youth said in his Sunday school class in a poem he wrote about God's creation: "When God created the whole universe, He took the sun and the moon and set them in their place. He took the stars and flung them in space, and He took the Earth and hung it in space. Then He told gravity to hold them in place, and gravity has been obeying God ever since."

There is much truth and wisdom in what this little boy said, for indeed, the force of gravity plays an important role in the universe. It is responsible for making it the way it is. It holds the planets of our solar system in place around the sun. It holds the other stars, planets, and galaxies in their proper places. We may not fully know "how," but we can safely say we know "why": because it is necessary to maintain the right environment for life here on earth.

There are several verses in the Bible that suggest that God continues to cause the universe to expand. Isaiah 40:22 KJV supports this concept: "He that sitteth upon the circle of the earth, and the inhabitants there [are] as grasshoppers; that *stretcheth out the heavens* as a curtain and spreadeth them out as a tent to dwell in" (emphasis mine). And in Jeremiah 10:12 KJV we read, "He hath made the earth by His power, He hath established the world by His wisdom, and hath stretched out the heavens by His discretion." (See also Psalm 104:2 NIV.) The words *stretcheth* and *spreadeth* are in the present tense. We can see that several of the Bible prophets and writers imply that God continues to create an expanding universe. Could it also be because some stars are burning out and therefore God creates new ones to sustain life on earth? Surely God knows.

As I continue to reflect on all that God has created, I am reminded of when I studied chemistry in college. I vividly recall having to memorize the chemical elements commonly known as the Periodic Table of Elements. In 1960 there were 102 elements listed in the table. Today there are 118 elements listed. Again, it is a reminder that man continues to discover new things in the universe. We are told in Ecclesiastes 1:9–10 NIV, "There is no new thing under the sun." Man may invent or discover new things, but the Creator is Jesus Christ. Meanwhile, although we may never know the full reason why the universe is expanding, we should be happy it is and know that God is too wise to make a mistake and too powerful to fail. So let us place our trust in God's wisdom.

Jesus Sustains and Controls the Whole Universe

It is fascinating to ponder the creation of the universe and recognize the magnitude of Jesus' ability as the Creator, sustainer, and controller of it and of life as we know it. The Bible tells us in Colossians 1:16 NIV that Jesus created everything in the universe by His power and that all things were created for His pleasure. Colossians 1:17 NIV says, "He [Jesus] is before all things, and in Him all things hold together." Jesus "is before all things," that is, He existed before any of the created things. If Jesus existed before all things existed, it means that He existed in eternity past. In other words, when the universe had its beginning, He was already there. In Colossians 1:17 NIV Paul also wrote that "by Him all things consist." It means that it is Jesus Christ who holds everything in the universe together: everything large, such as the solar system, the galaxies of stars, and even everything tiny such as the atoms are being held together by Him.

In Hebrews 1:3 KJV we are told that Jesus is "upholding all things by the word of His power." He has the ability to hold everything together and all that He has created in its proper place. Isn't it reassuring to know that everything in the universe, the heavens, and in the earth is kept by His power?

Isaiah 55:11 NIV says, "My word that goes out from my mouth; It will not return to me empty, but will accomplish what I desire, and achieve the purpose for which I sent it."

Job 12:10 NIV says, "In His hand is the life of everything and the breath of all mankind."

Hebrews 2:8 NIV tells us, "In putting everything in subjection under His feet, God left nothing that is not subject to Him. Yet at present we do not see everything subject to Him."

First Chronicles 29:11 NIV is what we all should proclaim: "Yours, O Lord, is the greatness and the power and the glory and the victory and the majesty, for all that is in the heavens and in

103

the earth is yours; Yours is the kingdom, O Lord, you are exalted as head over all."

Isn't it reassuring to know that Jesus did not create the universe and then just go away? He created it, and He sustains and controls it also.

We Are Joint Heirs with Jesus in His Kingdom and Universe

As we gaze at the stars, way up in the heavens, what do we see? The answer to this question is given to us by the apostle Paul in 1 Corinthians 2:9 NIV by the inspiration of God as it echoes what the prophet Isaiah had uttered some seven hundred years earlier: "However, as it is written, no ear has heard, no mind has conceived, what God has prepared for those who love Him." Our finite mind cannot fathom all that God has made for us in the universe.

Moreover, there are Christians today who have not fully grasped the meaning of all that we have inherited as joint heirs with Christ. I believe it is in part because we have, by and large, attempted to discover God's creation and who He is by exploring only that which is visible or can be measured.

Man is very limited in his earthen body by time and space, yet he has a desire to explore our universe. That innate drive has led us to discovering ways to fly in the air. That innate drive led to the Apollo space exploration program that landed a man on the moon in 1969, and as a result America continues to probe further into the universe, trying to find answers to the meaning and purpose of life. It is a fascination with creation that has continually caused other countries to follow suit: Russia, China, and Germany, and others as well.

Human beings have a fascination with the universe, and we should. Think about it: we are the crown of God's great creation.

Something about the stars in the heavens causes one to marvel at the magnitude of it all and yet wonder why God is mindful of mere man. King David attested to this very thought as he marveled at his place in the whole scheme of it all.

King David performed his duties as a young shepherd boy in Israel. Shepherd boys spent hours and hours alone in the open desert regions around the Judean Mountains. At night they had plenty of time to gaze up into the skies. As a shepherd boy, he was awed by the glory of the heavens night after night. He wrote in Psalm 8:3–4 NIV, "When I consider your heavens, the work of your fingers, the moon and the stars, which you have set in place, what is man that you are mindful of him, and the son of man that you care for him?"

What about you? Have you considered your place in the universe? As incredible as it may seem, the Bible says the earth and the universe were made for mankind. The order and purpose of creation in Genesis 1 and 2 attest to this truth. (See Genesis 1 and 2 on creation.)

David reminds us in Psalm 8:5–9 NIV that God gave us dominion over the physical earth and its creatures. God is preparing us to learn how to govern and to serve as faithful stewards right here on earth. Why is God giving us so much dominion over the earth? The answer is astounding, and many have not fully grasped this truth. But the Bible makes it clear: God is giving us the privilege to prepare for greater opportunity and stewardship in the future. The Scripture in Matthew 25:23 NIV reminds us what He said to His faithful servants: "Well done, my good and faithful servant. You have been faithful with a few things, I will put you in charge of many things."

God not only wants to give you dominion over the whole earth, but also wants to share the whole universe with you! But we can do that only when we inherit eternal life, when we become immortal children of God through Christ Jesus. What a motivational and awesome thought! Hebrews 2:7–8 NASB reveals this truth in quoting what David said in Psalm 8:5–9 NASB: "You have put all things in subjection under his [man's] feet." But let us remember, God gives us only designated authority and rulership, because He is still in charge. Yes, God has a plan and purpose for your life here and now, on earth, and a plan for you in the whole universe in the future. These are the promises that God gives us when we become heirs of God and joint heirs with Christ.

Hebrews 1:1–2 NIV reveals that God has appointed Jesus Christ the Creator and heir of all things: "In the past God spoke to our forefathers through the prophets at many times and in various ways, but in these last days, He has spoken to us by His Son, whom He has appointed heir of all things, and through whom He made the universe."

I used to read the Bible primarily to find out how to be a successful and victorious Christian. But now I read it to find out more about Jesus, because the more I know about Jesus, the more I know about our blessings in Him. Why is this so important? Second Peter 1:3 NLT tells us, "As we know Jesus better, His divine power gives us everything we need for living a godly life."

Today, God wants you to know that if you have been born again (John 3:3), you're no longer a "slave" to this world but a son of the Most High God. Notice what we are told in Galatians 4:7 NIV: "Now you are no longer a slave, but God's own child. And since you are His child, everything He has belongs to you." Paul expands on this mysterious truth in Romans 8:16–17 NIV: "The Spirit Himself testifies that we are God's children. Now if we are children, we are heirs—heirs of God and co-heirs of Christ." What a blessing it is to know that with Christ Jesus, you inherit everything He has!

Can you imagine this? Jesus is rich, and we are joint heirs with Him. It means that each one of us is rich. You may not have any money, but you're rich. You may not own houses or land, but you're rich. You may not have good health, but you're rich. You can be one of the richest people in the universe! It can happen today if you acknowledge Christ Jesus as your Savior. It's free, God's salvation by grace though faith. You can't buy it; you can't earn it. It's free!

Don't even think about counting all the riches of Jesus. They are unsearchable. Paul attests to this wonderful truth in Ephesians 3:8 NIV, where he wrote, "This grace was given me, to preach to the Gentiles the unsearchable riches of Christ." Think about it: no earthly inheritance can ever offer these riches. They can be found only in Christ Jesus, who is unsearchable. God wants to share these riches with you. They are yours for the asking!

God has a wonderful plan of salvation for all humanity, but He wants us to be a part of His family now, and in all eternity. Paul wrote in Ephesians 3:14–15 NIV, "For this reason I bow my knees to the Father of our Lord Jesus Christ, from whom the family in heaven and on earth is named."

Paul tells us in Colossians 1:13 KJV that the day we received Christ Jesus as our Savior, God translated us into His kingdom: "Who hath delivered us from the power of darkness, and has translated us into the kingdom of His dear Son." We, as Christians, have already been translated into the spiritual kingdom of God. But one day we will inherit the physical kingdom of God. The prophet in Daniel 7:18 NIV wrote, "But the saints of the Most High shall receive the kingdom, and possess it—yes, forever, and ever."

When Jesus came to this earth in the flesh, He reminded us that He was ushering in the spiritual kingdom. Jesus said in Matthew 4:17 KJV "Repent: for the kingdom of heaven is at hand."

In short, because Christ Jesus is the Creator of the universe, we can be partakers of all that He has created. It is Jesus who made it possible for all our needs on every level to be met. He is the source of all our needs: our physiological needs, our security needs, our social needs, our esteem needs, our self-actualization needs, and our spiritual self-actualization needs. And He places heroes in our life to make this possible. Remember: our highest level of need is the spiritual self-actualization need. And only Jesus Christ can make fulfillment of that need possible. He is able to make this possible because He is not only the Creator of the whole universe, but also the Savior. He is our greatest hero!

And finally, the Bible reveals to us why Jesus is able to be our Creator: He is God. Because He is God, He is qualified to be our Creator. Because He is God, He is qualified to be our Savior. Next, we will see why He is our Savior.

CHAPTER 13

Seeing Jesus Christ as Our
Savior, the Greatest Hero

Jesus Is Our Savior in the Natural Realm

When we think of the word *savior*, it reminds us of someone who saves, delivers, and rescues us or others from peril, danger, or calamity. And of course a cursory reading of the Old Testament tells us that God has repeatedly saved people from danger and destruction. Exodus 14:1–15:2 tells the familiar story of how God saved Israel at the Red Sea. The Israelites were trapped between the Egyptian army and the Red Sea. God caused the Red Sea to open so that they could cross over to the other side, and then caused it to close again and drown the pursuing Egyptian army.

In another example, God used David when he was just a little shepherd boy to defeat Goliath and his army to save Israel, as cited in 1 Samuel 17:32–58. Judges 7 tells us that God used Gideon and his army to defeat the Midianites. God deliberately reduced the size of Gideon's army so they would not think they had saved themselves by their own hand. These and other examples in the Old Testament and the Bible in general illustrate God delivering His people from danger.

As I look back on my life, I realize that God saved me from many dangerous circumstances, even those I can't remember. Oftentimes, God dispatches His angels to save us from hurt, harm, or danger. God has used other humans to deliver us from dangers, heroes from all walks of life. God is the ultimate Savior. He has the wherewithal to save us in all our circumstances, from the least to the greatest, in the natural realm of things.

Jesus Is Our Savior in the Spiritual Realm

Why does man need a Savior in the spiritual realm? The simple answer to this question is that man cannot save himself. Genesis 3 reveals to us that the sin problem began in the garden of Eden. Adam and Eve disobeyed God and thereby were separated from Him. Because of Adam and Eve's disobedience, sin entered into this world. And, as a consequence, everyone who is born into this world has inherited their sin nature. Romans 5:12 KJV says, "Wherefore, as by one man [Adam] sin entered into the world, and death by sin; and so death passed upon all men, for that all have sinned."

Thus, we all are born into this world separated from God, with no way to return to Him on our own. We need a Savior. We can't qualify as a savior because we are sinners. Romans 3:23 KJV reminds us of this regrettable truth: "For all have sinned, and come short of the glory of God." A wide gap separates man from God. Only Jesus can bridge that gap.

Romans 8:20–23 indicates that the whole of creation was affected and became corrupt through the fall of mankind into sin and is now waiting for redemption. In Colossians 1:20 KJV we are told, "And having made peace through the blood of His cross by Him to reconcile all things unto Himself; by Him, I say, whether they be things in earth, or things in heaven." In other words, one day God will restore all creation in the universe to what He intended it to be. This can never be done by man, a sinner and finite being. Only Jesus is able to do that, because He has all the qualifications.

Why Jesus Came to Save Us

God is a holy God. As a result of the sin of Adam and Eve, our first earthly parents, God knew that humankind had been separated from Him spiritually. Remember: God created us to have fellowship with Him. God is holy, but He is also a God of justice, and He has to punish sin and disobedience. However, He is a God of love. And because of His love for us, He prepared a way for us to return to Him. Jesus is the way.

In John 3:16 NIV we read, "For God so loved the world that He gave His one and only Son, that whoever believes in Him shall not perish but have eternal life." Jesus tells us in John 14:6 NIV, "I am the way and the truth and the life. No one comes to the Father except through me."

Why was it necessary for Jesus to come for us to be saved? Why couldn't man save himself? Once again, recall Romans 3:23 NIV, that "All have sinned and come short of the Glory of God." Man himself cannot qualify to be a savior in the spiritual realm, because he is a sinner.

Jesus is the only one who can qualify to be our Savior, because He is without sin. As it says in 2 Corinthians 5:21 KJV, "For He made Him who knew no sin to be sin for us, that we might become the righteousness of God in Him." Hebrews 4:15 NIV tells us, "For we do not have a high priest who is unable to sympathize with our weaknesses, but we have one who has been tempted in every way, just as we are---yet was without sin." Think about it: if Jesus had sinned once, it would have disqualified Him from being our Savior. He sinned not once, because He is God!

111

As it says in Romans 5:6–10, when we were without strength, helpless and unable to save ourselves, Christ died for the ungodly. This is how we can be saved from the ultimate punishment of God and be reconciled to Him. This is why Jesus had to come to earth as a man. Remember: as God, He could not die. But by becoming a man, He could suffer death and pay the penalty for our sins. He came as God-Man.

How Jesus Came to Save Us

No earthly hero can do what Jesus did. Before He came to earth, Jesus was in heaven with God the Father, enjoying all the glory and power of God. Think about it: here is Jesus the Creator in heaven. He knew His creatures on earth were disobedient and doomed to eternal punishment. But because of His compassion and love for us, He determined a way to avoid this for all who would be willing to accept salvation. Thank God He looked down on earth through His eyes of love and compassion and decided to come to us who need a way to be reconciled with God, so that we can live with Him forever in His heavenly kingdom. It was His love for us that led Jesus to leave the joys and privileges of heaven to come to earth and live as a man.

He took off His royal role and became a man so that He could redeem man. Notice what is written in Philippians 2:6–8 NIV: "Who, being in the very nature of God, did not consider equality with God something to be grasped, but made Himself nothing, taking the very nature of a servant, being made in human likeness. And being found in appearance as a man, he humbled himself and became obedient to death, even death on a cross!"

Isn't it amazing? He who was rich became poor so that we who are poor could become rich. It was His love that caused Him to do this; it was His love that motivated Him to leave the glory of heaven and come to earth, to show what it means to love God and one another. It was His love that showed us it is possible to live a life here on earth in a way that is pleasing to God.

But most of all it was His love that motivated Him to endure the agony of the cross so that we could be redeemed. And it was in the power of His resurrection that He rose from the grave. He lives today! Because He lives, we can live in the blessed hope that we, too, will live with Him one day.

Meanwhile, we wait until He returns again as we remember what He said in John 14:1–3 NIV: "Do not let your heart be troubled. Trust in God, trust also in me. In my Father's house are many rooms; if it were not so, I would have told you. I am going there to prepare a place for you. I will come back and take you to be with me that you also may be where I am." We can trust God because "He cannot lie" as it says in Titus 1:2. And His Word is truth (2 Timothy 2:15). Our God is a faithful God; if He says it, He will do it. God is preparing a place for us in His heavenly kingdom that encompasses the whole universe!

Before we can literally benefit from all that we have inherited with Jesus Christ in the whole universe, He has some unfinished business. He is coming back to earth to defeat Satan and all his followers, and to finally purge the whole universe from sin.

Again, remember what is said in Romans 8:22 NIV: "We know that the whole creation has been groaning as in the pain of childbirth right up this present time. Not only so, but we ourselves, who have the first fruits of the Spirit, groan inwardly as we wait eagerly for our adoption as sons, the redemption of our bodies." The whole of God's creation is waiting; we are waiting for His return. I don't know about you, but I am waiting with great expectation.

CHAPTER 14

Jesus' Final Preparation for Us to Live with Him as Joint Heirs in the Ultimate Heavenly Kingdom and Universe

After Jesus Christ has dealt with Satan and all His followers as cited in Isaiah 34 and 65 and Revelation 20:10, and after He has dwelt with all those whose names were not written in the "Lamb's Book of Life" at the great white throne judgment, He will purge and purify the whole universe from sin's effect.

Remember: Satan and the other fallen angels with him were cast out of heaven where God and his saints abided. We read in Revelation 12:10 that Satan and the other fallen angels were cast out of heaven where God lives, down to earth. Thus Satan and his fallen angels, now with no chance of redemption, polluted the second heaven, the stars and the moon, and the other hosts of the celestial space, and the first heaven (the atmospheric space, the skies above the earth). He has polluted the whole earth and its worldly system. As a result, God will purge the whole universe.

In 2 Peter 3:10 NIV we read, "But the day of the Lord will come as a thief in the night; in the which the heavens shall pass away with a great noise, and the elements shall melt with fervent heat, the earth also and the works that are therein shall be burned up."

Remember, it says in the creation chapters, Genesis 1 and 2, that God created all the stars in the universe and all the elements necessary for human and other life to exist in the physical realm. You perhaps recall that I mentioned the Periodic Table of the Elements, which is also called the Chemical Elements Chart. Isn't it interesting that in 2 Peter 3:10 it says that these "elements shall melt with fervent heat," meaning they will no longer exist in their initial state?

I recall learning in my science and chemistry classes that matter is anything that has weight and occupies space. I also recall being told that matter cannot be destroyed; rather it can only be changed into another form. Only God knows the extent to which these elements melt, but what is very clear is that God in the last days of the universe as we know it will change the order of things to prepare new heavens and a new earth—that is, a new universe within His heavenly kingdom for our future spiritually glorified bodies.

The prophet Isaiah wrote in the Old Testament, Isaiah 65:17–18 NIV "Behold, I will create new heavens and a new earth. The former will not be remembered, nor will they come to mind. But be glad and rejoice forever in what I will create, for I create Jerusalem to be a delight and its people a joy. I will rejoice over Jerusalem and take delight in my people; the sound of weeping and of crying will be heard in it no more."

The psalmist in Psalm 102:25–27 NIV wrote, "In the beginning you laid the foundations of the earth, and the heavens are the work of your hands. They will perish, but you will remain; they will all wear out like a garment. Like clothing you will change them, and they will be discarded. But you remain the same. And your years will never end."

The apostle Peter wrote in the New Testament, 2 Peter 3:10 KJV, "But the day of the Lord will come as a thief in the night; in the which the heavens [the atmospheric sky, and celestial spaces, stars, and so on] shall pass away with a great noise, and the *elements* shall melt with fervent heat, the earth also and the works that are therein shall be burnt up" (emphasis mine). Remember, when all this is going on, we, the redeemed, will be in our spiritually glorified bodies with the Lord.

Now notice what John tells us he saw in Revelation 21:1–4 NIV.

> "Then I saw a new heaven and a new earth, for the first heaven and the first earth had passed away, and there were no longer any sea. I saw the Holy City, the New Jerusalem, coming down out of heaven from God, prepared for a bride beautifully dressed for her husband. And I heard a loud voice from the throne saying, 'Now the dwelling of God is with men, and He will live with them and be their God. They will be His people, and God Himself will be with them and be their God. He will wipe every tear from their eyes. There will be no more death or mourning or crying or pain, for the old order of things has passed away.'"

When I read the phrase in Revelation 21:4 NIV *coming down out of heaven from God,* I think about a time when I was riding in an elevator from the first floor to a floor higher up. A little boy was riding on the elevator with us. As he looked through the elevator's window, he saw the buildings outside moving. He made an innocent observation as he said, "Look at all those buildings coming down past us."

Another time I was flying in a passenger jet airliner from Long Island to Birmingham, Alabama. A little girl was sitting in a seat behind me, and as she looked out through the airplane's window, she saw the clouds passing by. She said with innocent excitement, "Mama, look: the clouds are coming at us!" It may seem funny to us, but the little boy on the elevator and the little girl on the airplane didn't know that in reality the elevator was moving up and the airplane was moving forward. Nor did they realize they were experiencing an optical illusion.

I often ask myself when I read what the apostle John said, "I saw the Holy City coming down from God out of heaven," could it be that the earth was moving up toward heaven? Of course, the answer I always come up with is that God knows, and whatever He does is always perfect. Think about it: God owns the whole universe. He will not destroy the universe, rather, He will purge it, and change the order of things. God's heavenly kingdom includes the whole universe and the earth within it! He owns it all! As He has promised in the Scriptures, we are joint heirs with Jesus Christ! We are rich!

Jesus will use the earth as His headquarters. We will live with Him forever and have access to all of God's heavenly kingdom, His universe. We then will have spiritually glorified body just like His. Remember what the apostle John said in 1 John 3:2 NIV, "Beloved, now are we the children of God, and it does not yet appear what we shall be: but we know that, when He shall appear, we shall be like Him; for we shall see Him as He is."

Consider this with me: We will no longer be limited by time or space. We will be able to travel throughout the whole universe. What a day that will be! Can you imagine all the unspeakable blessings waiting for us? Who would not want to be joint heirs with Jesus Christ? Who would not want to have riches unknown? If I were you, I wouldn't wait another moment. Ask Him to come into your life right now and He will make you His child so that you, too, can become a joint heir with Him, and so that you, too, can become one of the richest people in the world!

When you commit your life to Him, it will never be the same. Your life will begin to have new purposes. When Jesus comes into your life, you will, both now and in the future, be a partaker of all of Jesus' divine blessings in both the natural and the spiritual realm.

When you allow this to happen, you will, as I have discovered, gain entrance into the sphere of spiritual blessings that will continually help you grow in the spiritual self-actualization stage, one that will permeate your other needs: physiological needs, security needs, social needs, esteem needs, and self-actualization needs. He will supply all your needs!

This is what I learn more and more every day, after having totally committed my life to Jesus and studied the Scriptures, allowing God's inspired Word to reveal to me that Jesus is the Creator of the universe and everything therein, and that He is our Savior. In addition, Jesus is qualified to be our Creator and Savior because He is God! It is my prayer that you, as I did, will come to realize that He is the Creator of the universe as well as our Savior. When you allow this to happen, you will be able to say with me, "There is no one like Jesus. He is the greatest hero!"

When you put Him first, all your needs will be met. Matthew 6:33 KJV says, "But seek first His kingdom and His righteousness and all these things will be given to you as well." When we put Him first, we can be assured that in meeting our needs, He is the source and ultimate provider, in both the natural and spiritual realm.

May we never forget that God comes to man through man. He empowers others from every walk of life to be heroes in our lives, to help meet our needs, as we sojourn on earth. And don't forget, He calls on you and me to be heroes for others, too.

Finally, I cannot emphasize this enough: we need to look beyond how the media and others define heroes. We must not allow society to define our heroes for us, establishing the parameters or boundaries by which a hero is defined. Again, may I suggest that you need to define your own heroes, because it is you as an individual who experiences them with your own eyes and ears … through your five senses and, yes, through your spiritual sense, throughout your life journey. Let no one else decide for you. Only you know the people who have influenced your life in a positive way.

I encourage you to take time each day and reflect on your life; then you will discover who your real heroes are. This is what I have discovered in my search for heroes. They come from all walks of life, most often from the ranks of ordinary people.

When you allow this to happen, you will discover those real heroes who have made a difference in your life. And for the most part, you will discover that they include your mother, your father, that teacher, that preacher, that farmer, that soldier, that politician, that stranger; rich or poor people from every walk of life; someone who said something to you or did something for you that encouraged or helped you to move forward in life.

Most of all, take time out to thank God for being God and the greatest hero. Give thanks to those whom God has empowered to help you. When you begin to do this, when you begin to live your life with an attitude of gratitude, your life will have joy, peace, happiness and purpose in it like never before. When you allow this to happen you can discover that you serve a cause greater than "self." It is a cause that must begin and end with God. And as you recognize God as the source of that cause, He will direct your paths.

Don't let negative experiences in your life hold you back. Rather, keep searching for heroes in your life, people who are positive, people who encourage you to go forward.

Be a bridge builder. There is a story about an old man who was traveling through life. When he crossed the final river in his life, he turned around and built a bridge over the river. A stranger came by and said, "Old man, why are you building a bridge over the river? You have already crossed it." The old man lifted his gray head and said, "Yes, my friend, it's true I have already crossed this river. But you see, I am building a bridge for that bright-eyed youth who may have to cross this river one day. My friend, I am building it for him." Think about it: Jesus is not only our greatest hero but the greatest bridge builder. He is building a bridge for you right now! And He calls on each one of us to be bridge builders.

So I say to you today that with Christ Jesus on your side, your future is getting brighter every day. May you always remember, there is a bright side somewhere; there is a bright side somewhere. Don't you rest until you find it!

Don't let negative people or circumstances hold you down. And never forget: Searching for heroes in life is sometimes like searching for precious pearls. You can find them if you dig deep enough.

Quit letting negative circumstances or negative people hold you back; quit having self-pity parties. Lift your head off your chest. Rise up and go on. For you are rich; you are a joint heir with Christ! Your future is bright!

Let positive thinking rule your life.

"Finally, brothers and sisters. Whatever is true, whatever is noble, whatever is right, whatever is pure, whatever is lovely, whatever is admirable—If anything is excellent or praiseworthy— think about such things" (Philippians 4:8 NIV).

Keep searching for heroes in your life, keep moving forward, and be a hero in the life of others.

The End